Praise for

"Dizzyingly well researched... This book is a great reference on the in and outs of economics, politics, finance and the human condition."

– Alternatives Journal

"An easily-accessible and thought-provoking book."

– Elizabeth May,
Leader of the Green Party of Canada

"Andrew Welch voices the concern – and examines the causes – that many of us have but cannot articulate as well as he does: that human values everywhere are decaying at an alarming rate. [...] This is a thought-provoking book that you should read, act upon, and share."

– Tapestry Magazine

THE VALUE CRISIS

THE VALUE CRISIS

From Dollars to Democracy,
Why Numbers are Ruining Our World

Andrew Welch

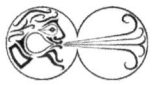

Aanimad Press

Second Edition

Editing by Mirjam Urfer and Michele Fisher
Cover design by Sheila Britton
Illustrations property of the author.

www.TheValueCrisis.com

First edition: August, 2014
Second printing: October, 2015

Library and Archives Canada Cataloguing in Publication Data

Welch, Andrew, 1962-

The value crisis : from dollars to democracy, why numbers are ruining our world / by Andrew
Welch

ISBN 978-0-9879105-0-9 (pbk)

1. Ecological economics   2. Economic philosophy   3. Human ecology   I. Title

Published by Aanimad Press
57 Mary Street
Caledon, Ontario
L7K 0E3
Canada
(416) 907-2076

CONTENTS

Foreword

THE BOOK IN YOUR HANDS provides valuable insight into the challenge of our times.

The basic challenge has been clear since the early 1970s. With the first oil crisis, added to Rachel Carson's revelation that manufactured chemicals can disrupt life, it began to dawn on some that the continued expansion of human activity was changing our relationship with the Earth. That change, from insignificance to big disruptive influence has now taken place, and ever more frequently we are feeling the repercussions.

For thousands of years, having more people and more powerful technologies have led to more secure and satisfying lives for large numbers of people. Consequently, most countries have established customs and institutions to encourage further growth. Today, unfortunately, continued expansion is the source of our greatest problems.

Real growth has been rare in the developed world ever since new frontiers to grow into became scarce. Most 'growth' over the last decade has been an illusion spun by creative paperwork in financial markets. Trillions of dollars in stimulus and bail-out money has had little success in advancing real growth.

Over the years, experience has shown that if an economy is not growing, many people fall on hard times. This suggests that growth is necessary. Not so, I discovered. We only suffer when the economy isn't growing because of the way our monetary system is set up. There are other ways to manage mutual provision - the essential function of economics.

Societies now need to maintain a stable balance within the Earth's ability to support them. This requires a very different goal from that of days gone by when we had vast new territories to grow into.

How do we change our goal as a society?

The first step is understanding. In <u>Life, Money and Illusion</u> I wrote about why the present system requires perpetual expansion, how our

7

relationship with the Earth has changed, and how human culture might evolve to accommodate that change. In <u>The Value Crisis</u> Andrew Welch adds an important element to the understanding needed for society to shed its caterpillar skin and emerge as the butterfly that human culture is capable of becoming. He provides an explanation for why we are responding so slowly to the challenges at hand.

The global crisis we are in is greatly aggravated by the fact that numbers are precise, easily understood, and when compared or combined in specific ways, always lead to the same conclusions. Two plus two equals four in all languages and cultures. The philosophy of letting markets make society's choices is based on prices, expressed as numbers. In the face of such clarity, the values of friendship, long-term well-being, justice and the like, with their lack of precise measurements, have been usurped by the market faith for making decisions. The awareness needed to reclaim social and environmental valuation in decision-making is a part of what this book offers.

Another problem with our number-based value system is that it has no place for "enough". While one can have enough food, clothes, shelter and the like, numbers go on infinitely. There is no end to the amount of money one might aspire to. The present system can never arrive, even as unimaginably huge numbers accumulate in accounts and our only planet is drained of its vitality.

Andrew Welch has pinpointed the conceptual bottleneck of a value system that cannot serve us in our new circumstances. As individuals, the present system casts us in the roles of consumers or investors. Both roles are defined by trying to get as much as possible with our money. These numerically-based values often conflict with our older role as citizens in which we based decisions on the well-being of other people, the future, and the life around us.

By grasping the message of this book, you can help enable our culture to flow more smoothly toward better outcomes.

Mike Nickerson
author of <u>Life, Money and Illusion</u>
http://www.SustainWellBeing.net

Introduction

I LOVE NUMBERS, AND ALWAYS HAVE. One of the very few memories I have of my early childhood is a recitation of the even numbers from 2 to 30 at school. I was the first child in my Grade 1 class to complete this task and was thus allowed to go and play with the plastic farm animals in the toy section while my classmates worked on the sequence. A decade later, I was the kind of eager high school math student who pursued sideline interests in numbers for their own sake. I recall filling a few pages of a notebook with a compilation of numbers known as Pascal's Triangle, and then filling more pages with lists of the patterns that I was able to find in that construction. As you might imagine, not many of my classmates shared my enthusiasm for such purely numerical pursuits, but I enjoyed the exploration.

Throughout high school, I was enthralled by the objectivity of numbers and number-based studies, but the 'arbitrary' nature of writing held no appeal at all. In fact, when I decided to pursue mathematics at the University of Waterloo, I distinctly recall hoping that once I left high school my essay-writing days would be over. Never again would I be searching for sentences or struggling to formulate thoughts into paragraphs. It seemed so much easier and more 'valid' to do work that was either right or wrong, and not subject to the whims and opinions of the instructor who was grading my effort.

Needless to say, my attitude towards writing has changed over the years, but it is only recently that I have begun to question my original assumptions about numbers as well. As someone who respects science and nature, I could not ignore the overwhelming evidence of environmental degradation, climate change, and biodiversity loss. As a consumer and investor, I faced the reality of skyrocketing energy prices, economic meltdowns, and the threat of worse yet to come. As a conscientious citizen, I was disturbed by the injustice of income disparity and the flaws of unpopular democracies. And yet, I could clearly see how the objective numbers of profit, economic growth, and the relentless pursuit of wealth could easily justify all of our enabling choices as rational, worthy decisions.

While we all see the urgency of the multiple global crises looming on the horizon, there's a disconnect between the consequences and our present behaviours. Actions that most likely caused our current predicament not only continue, we seem to be desperately striving for their unhindered acceleration. We use debt to conjure up trillions of dollars from nothing; we voraciously run through our planet's limited resources; and we recklessly contaminate our environment with waste, by-products, and dangerous substances. The train is heading off the rails and still we can't help but madly shovel coal into the boiler. Could our reliance on numbers to measure value be responsible for our single-minded complacency?

I had grown up believing that numbers held the answers to humanity's every difficulty. If we could set aside our irrational emotions and focus on the facts, all could be made right. However, it seems that the more 'rational' we become, the worse things get.

- Why do we have to consume and throw out so much stuff?

- Why do certain individuals get paid so much money for doing so little?

- Why do we seem to have less time than previous generations, not more?

- Why does it cost more to repair things than to replace them?

- Why are labour disruptions, disliked on all sides, still common?

- Why do we in democracies disagree so much with our elected leaders and governments?

- Why do we consciously choose to poison our own natural environment?

- Why are so many of us not even sure what makes us happy anymore?

This book proposes answers to these questions by exploring the inter-section of two potent concepts: *values* and *numbers*. Values determine our behaviours, both individually and collectively. They allow us to evaluate and prioritize options in order to make decisions. In today's world, we make decisions using two very different kinds of value systems: *human value systems*, which are as old as our species, and *number-based value systems*, which developed much later in our history. Human values include our survival impulses, cultures, beliefs, morals, welfare, and happiness; they are qualitative by nature. Number-based values, on the other hand, are exclusively measured by numeric quantity – money being the most common example.

Have you ever wondered why unions and management are able to sit down and resolve their differences, whereas commercial interest groups and environmentalists seem incapable of even talking to one another? The difference is one of values. In a labour dispute both sides are operating within the same value system – a number-based one. As a result, they both want the same thing – a larger slice of the pie. This mutual understanding allows them to grasp each other's motivations. Business people and environmentalists, on the other hand, are eval-uating the state of the world and its future using completely different and fundamentally incompatible value systems. This *crisis of values* is in fact the greatest challenge that we now face as a global society.

The most important difference between the two systems is that numbers are inherently linear and limitless. That means that within a strictly numeric scale, there is no concept of "enough" or "too much". Any value that is measured by number – a person's possible net worth, for example – is unbounded; you can always add more. Thus, any undertaking which aims to maximize such a value is a never-ending quest. That fundamental trait is what gets us into trouble.

We have created huge corporations that, by design, operate exclu-sively under number-based values. As their power and influence grows, societal assets that do not appear on corporate balance sheets are rapidly consumed or crushed in the unending quest for profit maximization. Even our governments are based on numbers: be it how our policy-makers are selected (election), how they make decisions (majority vote), or what they use as their measure of success (statistical indices).

The apparent simplicity and objectivity of numbers are why we take their influence for granted. They greatly streamline the processes of decision-making and progress measurement. Consequently, number-based value systems are increasingly adopted as the *only* measures of value – even for situations in which using human values would be more appropriate. Our human values are being displaced.

As a mathematician raised in the halls of business and science, I understand how number-based thinking works. I suggest that the number-based value systems we have relied upon to drive our phenomenal progress and prosperity have unacknowledged flaws. Their boundless linearity demands constant growth in order to achieve constant value increases. While economic growth is the unquestioned goal of both the private and public sectors, sustaining it is impossible based on our current model of resource consumption. Even though we haven't run out of everything (yet), there is valid concern that we have already exceeded the capacity of our limited planetary resources to fuel our present wealth, which mainly exists as debt. We are now borrowing heavily from our future.

Some people attribute our looming crises to phenomenal greed or short-sightedness, while others attribute them to indifference or societal habits too deeply ingrained to change. I propose that what we are facing is not a crisis of selfishness or apathy, but rather a crisis of incompatible and unbalanced value forces. Society has evolved to the point where number-based value systems like money are needed to manage our immediate needs (by spending) and our future needs (by saving), but there are also the needs of others and the needs of the planet to be considered. These needs can only be met by exercising human values – by giving wealth away, by foregoing profit, by honouring the necessity of compassion, culture, justice, the environment, and diversity. Spending, saving, and giving are each the result of distinct value systems, all of which are in constant conflict. This book will explain why those conflicts are responsible for our inability to take effective action in response to some of the toughest challenges that civilization has ever confronted.

This is primarily a book of ideas, not one filled with historical facts and footnotes. Where examples are given, they are used to illustrate and clarify concepts rather than to prove assertions. The book does not overwhelm with economic theory, detailed case histories, or statistics. If an absence of the latter suggests that the arguments lack validity, then my work has already begun.

Naturally I have borrowed theories and insights from others, while a number of other proposals came out of my own struggles with the problems I was describing. It was both humbling and vindicating to discover that some of my 'new' ideas have in fact been well-known for the last century to a small group of economists, and that an entire branch of thought, *ecological economics*, is now devoted to them. This book is not an introduction to ecological economics, but I hope it makes a clear case for why we should all be more familiar with ecological economic principles. The book is also part of a personal journey – one in which I continue to wrestle with my own values, habits, and conscience. Each chapter includes personal anecdotes and reflections, which have greatly contributed to the theories that I present. My key ideas appear as boxed text and these also are summarized, starting on page 211.

Solutions to global challenges or even to the value crisis itself were not my primary objective in putting these thoughts to paper. My goal from the outset was to propose explanations for why we are failing to react to the imminent threats to civilization as we know it. Identifying the real reasons for previously inexplicable behaviours is the first step towards change, both personal and global.

Finally, the book advances a few idealistic alternatives to some deeply ingrained old ways of thinking. It is my hope that this work will open up unique avenues of exploration, provoke a broader conception of what might be possible, and inspire a useful new way of thinking about the enormous challenges that we face.

Andrew Welch
Caledon, Ontario, 2014

More than any other causal system with which science now concerns itself, the human value factor is going to determine the future.
– Roger Sperry, neuropsychologist (1913–1994)

Introduction to Second Edition

S EVEN YEARS HAVE PASSED SINCE the first edition of this book came out. I have learned a great deal in that time, from speaking to groups and hearing their feedback and also from voraciously working my way through the many other books that have been recommended to me along the way.

I am very pleased to be able to still stand behind my original hypothesis: that there are two distinct ways of measuring success, and that by giving incredible precedence to the quantitative measures of value, we have suffered from the unique properties of numbers that don't match our qualitative world. As you'll soon discover, numeric values, where more is always worth more, have no concept of sufficiency, so we never know when we have enough.

There was one section in Chapter 3 that needed some revision. It seems I gave the practice of barter undue significance in the history of money. I hope this edition more accurately reflects the role it played.

Also new to this edition is the addition of a simple index, allowing readers to not only reference topics but also to quickly access favourite anecdotes, stories, or quotes. The ability and opportunity to share these ideas with others is important; indeed significant interest was expressed by various book clubs to take up the work in some detail. In response, we created questions and free book clubs sets available for loan where practical. Please contact us if you're interested.

One frequent piece of feedback is that the book does a good job of describing the value crisis but lacks solutions. Readers ask what can be done, either as individuals or as a society to make a difference. While solutions were neither in my original intent nor in my scope of knowledge at the time, my research focus has since changed and I'm excited to announce that a sequel is now available, called: Our Second Chance – Changing Course and Solving the Value Crisis. It was first completed in March, 2020 – just before the world was thrown into lockdown by a novel coronavirus. As such, it was pulled back and completely reworked within the context of our new post-pandemic world. One thing definitely made apparent throughout that process is that COVID-19 put the value crisis into very clear perspective. It has never been easier to see where society is struggling and what is at the core of those struggles.

Andrew Welch
December, 2021

Chapter One

The Rise of Numbers

Although he may not always recognize his bondage,
modern man lives under a tyranny of numbers.
– Nicholas Eberstadt, political economist

H OW SAFE IS YOUR CAR? Today's motor vehicles have many outstanding safety features that all improve your odds of surviving an accident. Some are mandated by government regulation, while others are added to improve the marketability of the model. Could your car be made safer? Of course it could. Any product can be made safer. So how does a manufacturer decide when a car is safe enough? Do they base it on due diligence? Design trials? Market perception? These factors are all difficult to evaluate. However, by employing some simple numbers and statistics, such decisions actually become terrifyingly straightforward, as the world learned to its shock in 1998.

In the preceding two decades, General Motors was experiencing a disproportionately high volume of lawsuits pertaining to vehicle fires. Accident victims were being killed by the ignition of their own gasoline, and the prevailing theory was that the design of GM cars and their gas tank placement was at fault. One case in particular involved six passengers who were severely burned when their Chevrolet Malibu exploded after a rear impact in 1993. That court battle dragged on for years until an incredible memo came to light.

The memorandum was titled "Value Analysis of Auto Fuel Fed Fire Related Fatalities" and had been prepared in 1973 by Ed Ivey, a young GM analyst working on fuel systems for their Oldsmobile division. With an estimated 500 fatalities resulting from fuel-fed fires in GM cars per year, the company already suspected that there was a problem and they wanted to know if a change was required for future models. From a government study, Ivey estimated that if GM was found liable, each fatality would cost the company about $200,000 in legal damages. Knowing that about 11% of these accidents would be in current model cars, and knowing the number of new cars built in a year, Ivey produced a formula which was stunning in its simplicity:

$$\frac{55 \text{ fatalities} \times \$200,000/\text{fatality}}{5,000,000 \text{ new model autos}} = \$2.20/\text{new model auto}$$

The same formula, when applied to 500 fatalities against all 41 million GM cars on the road per year came to a cost of $2.40 per car. Subsequent analysis indicated that the cost to fix the problem came to about $8.59 per vehicle. Thus the decision became trivial: The cost far outweighed the benefit, and GM chose the deaths of 500 customers per year over the reduction in profits to fix the issue.

This is an example of what economists call *cost-benefit analysis*, some variation of which lies at the core of nearly every decision we make. What made this particular application so abhorrent to the courts was how the costs and benefits were apparently being evaluated in such a cold and inhumane manner. And yet, in reality, that analytical application of numbers is unquestionably the norm. I can assure you that at this very moment, your government is using exactly the same calculations with respect to climate change, the economy, and the next election.

Indeed, I'll go even further and say that the prevalence of number-based values in decision-making is not just a characterization of our response to modern-day challenges. I argue that the fundamental principles of numbers are what have led to our present predicament of converging economic, social, and environmental disasters.

The very suggestion that numbers are responsible for any societal crisis may at first seem ridiculous. How can we blame numbers for an economic collapse? Numbers only *describe* things – they don't *cause* anything. When it comes to an environmental or energy crisis, don't scientists and technologists use numbers to make us aware of those threats and plan for a tactical response? True – numbers are what they are and they can be indispensable for problem-solving. However, *values* based on numbers are something quite different. Values *do* cause things to happen, sometimes with potentially disastrous consequences.

Before we delve into the many ways that number-based values influence our world, let's take a step back. Let's go to the time before numbers and see how they evolved, why they're unique, and what they mean to us in our lives today.

The Evolution of Numeracy

Numeracy is the ability to reason using numbers and other mathematical concepts. It is often thought of as simply the numeric version of *literacy*, the ability to read and write. However, there's an important difference between literacy and numeracy: Literacy is limited to humans; numeracy is not.

To demonstrate how numeracy has evolved over thousands of years to the place it holds in our society today, I have divided its progression into five general stages.

Birds, Bees, and 1-2-3s

The first stage of numeracy is one that seems to be part of our genetic wiring. It is the ability to distinguish and compare quantities of objects. While it is easy to imagine that the ability to determine more versus less would be favoured by evolution, it may be surprising to learn that a wide variety of living creatures – including fish, primates, salamanders, rats, birds, and even bees – have unexpected numeracy skills.

Experiments have shown that many animals can precisely identify a certain number of objects on sight, the limit of which varies by species. While salamanders seem able to distinguish quantities up to a limit of 3, bees have a limit of 4 or 5. Interestingly, humans have a similar limit of recognizing quantities. Unless objects are arranged in some familiar pattern like dots on a die, humans on average recognize no more than four objects visually. Beyond this, most people have to resort to sequential counting. Whether or not animals can 'count' objects in the same way or group them into parts and add them up is open to debate; what is clear is that many can recognize a particular quantity of objects instantly.

Animals also exhibit an ability to estimate relative proportion and size, with one interesting limitation: Reliable success only happens when the greater quantity is at least twice as big as the smaller one. This ratio is surprisingly consistent across species. So salamanders that can distinguish between 2 and 3 (using small number recognition) or between 5 and 10 (using relative comparison) cannot reliably distinguish between 4 and 6, or between 8 and 12. The prevailing theory is that separate brain functions are used to recognize quantity and determine proportion. Experiments with six-month-old infants show that the same cognitive separation is present in humans, suggesting that these two distinct numeracy skills have deep roots in our evolutionary history. These innate abilities are enhanced in some animals. For instance, primates have demonstrated sequential counting up to 9 and baby chicks have even performed very simple arithmetic – correctly determining that $1 + 2$ is greater than $4 - 2$!

To Infinity and Beyond

The second stage of numeracy begins to separate humans from animals. It is defined by using visual or linguistic symbols (like numbers) to represent quantities, so that any quantity can be precisely described from one person to the next. Early humans had a much smaller set of working numbers than we do today, running from "1" to some higher number, for example "10". (I term this the culture's *conceivable maximum*.) After that, the concept of "many" would likely have been a sufficient descriptor for our bands of ancestors to survive. In some cases, the systems were as simple as "one, two, and many". (The Pirahã language of Brazil still has this characteristic today.) As civilization progressed, and bands evolved into communities and societies, the *conceivable maximum* went up. By Roman times, 1000 ("M") was the highest value symbol required in their counting system. To describe the countless and the infinite – like the number of stars in the sky – classical Greeks created the word "myriad", a term that we still use today. Interestingly, "myriad" was also their word for 10,000.

The power of numbers is instilled in us at a very early age, as is our fascination with numbers that push our sense of bounds. I have a nephew who, at the age of three, exclaimed that, "Granddad is really old. He's... like... sixteen!" For someone my nephew's age, sixteen was a very high number. It seems that the evolution of society's increasing conceivable maximum is recapitulated in childhood development. Anyone who has ever led a group of children on a school field trip will be familiar with the questions children ask to seek wonder in the world around them: "How much does this weigh?" "What does this cost?" "How tall is that?" "How many are there?" They are hoping to get an answer back which will be fantastically high – thereby pushing their own conceivable maximum beyond its current limit. To be told that the object you are looking at weighs 38,000 pounds is to be able to conceive of an actual physical representation of that number. As a consequence, the number 38,000 has a bit more meaning to you in the real-world sense, instead of being just an abstract concept. The same thing happens when lengths and areas are described in the proverbial unit of football fields.

The quest to push the numeric boundaries of our minds has resulted today in conceivable maximums that are in every other sense *inconceivable*. We now have numbers and words which represent the atoms in the universe: between 10^{79} and 10^{81} – less than a *googol*, which is 10^{100} (1 followed by 100 zeroes). Atoms may still be in fact uncountable, but for any moment in time we consider them to be finite in number. Even more down-to-earth numbers, casually tossed around on the daily news, are largely inconceivable to the listeners. How many of us can properly grasp the consequential difference between a national debt of 17 billion dollars and a national debt of 1.7 trillion dollars, except as some math trivia? These numbers are conceptually unreal to most of us, and this is a profoundly important realization.

The Invention of Math

Advances in the second stage of numeracy, in which names are given to numbers and symbols are created to record them, were largely inspired by the needs of describing wealth and ownership. As civilization evolved further, the demands of commerce, trade, and taxation required

21

an ever-expanding list of numbers and some simple math to manipulate them. Thus began the third stage of numeracy: the development of arithmetical operations.

This stage, like the second, is a function of societal evolution rather than a survival imperative. Numbers and arithmetic must be taught, a trait that they have in common with literacy. They also both have concepts that can easily surpass our intuitive comprehension. It's not just very large numbers that we have trouble with. Some arithmetical operations, even in their most natural context, are foreign to how we think.

Consider the simple concept of growth: Anything that grows at a consistent and steady rate (expressed as a percentage) exhibits what is known as *exponential growth* – a very common mathematical concept. For example, at the end of every year, a population with a 6% annual growth rate will be 6% bigger than it was in the previous year. Anything with constant exponential growth, regardless of the quoted rate, will have a *doubling time* – the period of time in which the quantity repeatedly doubles. This concept is widespread throughout nature. However, there are some classic examples of how we are commonly unable to grasp exponential growth in our minds. I share two of them here.

The first is an old tale about an inventor in India (or Persia) who creates the game of chess. The ruler of the country is so taken with this game that he asks the inventor to name his price for it. The inventor presents a chessboard to the ruler and simply asks for a single grain of rice on the first square, two grains on the second square, four on the third, and so on, doubling the quantity for every square. The ruler accepts this deal, only to later discover that the resulting total amount of rice – more than 461 billion metric tons – would form a pile larger than Mount Everest.

The second is from a parable told by Canadian environmentalist David Suzuki: Imagine that you put a single bacterial cell in a test tube full of food. This particular bacterium divides every minute, resulting in two bacteria which continue to eat and, one minute later, divide into two themselves. Let us suppose that there is sufficient food in the test tube for this growth to continue for a full hour before the food is all gone and the test tube is filled with starving bacteria. When is half of the food gone? Most people are surprised to realize that half of the food still remains after 59 minutes. The population will double in the last minute, consuming the other half of the food!

Even after 55 minutes, the population is only at 3% of capacity and 97% of the starting food is still available to those cells. Imagine if at that point one bacterium were to announce to the others that in five minutes all of the food would be gone and the colony was doomed. Assuming that the other bacteria had the same level of innate numeracy that we have, that radical little cell would likely have been scoffed at and dismissed as a total alarmist. "What are you talking about? We've been here for nearly an hour with no problems! And look at all the food we have!"

Dr. Suzuki uses this parable to describe the limited amount of resources on our planet, and how, in his opinion, endless economic growth – far from being a necessity – is actually impossible, suicidal to pursue, and can collapse unexpectedly. Despite the most compelling evidence, most of us can't assimilate the math enough to intuitively reach the same conclusions and act accordingly.

> *The greatest shortcoming of the human race is our inability*
> *to understand the exponential function.*
> *– Albert A. Bartlett, physicist (1923–2013)*

This failure of all but the most mathematically-inclined humans to easily comprehend such functions and make rational decisions when faced with them is further exemplified by our widely varying ability in financial management. Compound interest, such as that applied to credit card debt, is an exponential function that can result in a balance owed that doubles every four years. Is it any wonder that the gap between the world's richest and poorest populations is widening at such a staggering rate?

Mathematicians and Mystical Powers

Even if we can't innately grasp huge numbers or exponential growth, there is a section of the population that has learned to comfortably work with these concepts: mathematicians. The fourth stage of numeracy is characterized by specialized individuals, performing math that goes beyond the scope of commerce or wealth measurement.

At first, such abstract explorations involved discoveries by induction: tinkering with numbers, observing the results, and deriving useful rules from such observations. For example, *Pythagorean triples* (like 3, 4, and 5, where $3^2 + 4^2 = 5^2$) are extremely useful for building structures with right angles. By applying such rules to everyday problems, great advances took place in engineering, navigation, resource management, and more. Another powerful application of math, when you start using it outside of the marketplace, is its predictive power. Once the patterns of natural phenomena such as eclipses are quantified, they can be predicted ahead of time – an amazing feat that was not possible before. Armed with such formulas and proofs, mathematicians could then perform deeds such as predicting the trajectory of cannon balls and the like – conveying a huge wartime advantage.

Arthur C. Clarke once wrote, "…any sufficiently advanced technology is indistinguishable from magic." The same might be said about sufficiently advanced math, for, to the uninitiated, it was presumed that mysterious powers were at work. Blending superstition with math, it wasn't long before people attributed numbers with mystical properties. Astrology, numerology, lucky numbers, biorhythms, and all manner of 'number worship' arose, aspects of which persist today. For example, we all know 666 as "The Number of the Beast", but long before it was appropriated by Christianity, it was widely known to mathematicians as being the sum of the natural numbers from 1 to 36 and also the sum of the squares of the first seven prime numbers.

This curious phenomenon, in which specific numbers are imbued with an added meaning – good or bad, lucky or unlucky – is visible in our daily lives all around the world. Just as many streets in the West have no houses numbered 13 and many buildings have no 13th floor, the absence of a 4th floor is quite common in Hong Kong. (The Cantonese word for "death" sounds similar to their word for "4".) In 2003, China's Sichuan Airlines purchased the rights to the 'very lucky' phone number 8888 8888 for 2.33 million yuan ($280,000), as the Cantonese word for "8" sounds like the word for "fortune". More recently, a Thai business man paid a record 11 million baht ($360,000) for an auspicious license plate reading "สส 9999" – "ส" means woman, while the Thai word for "9" is a homonym for a word meaning "stepping forward".

While it is easy to laugh off such customs as mere superstition, the power assigned to these numbers is tangible, as is their monetary value. Substantial riches are shelled out, based solely on the perceived value of certain numbers.

Civilization-by-Numbers

Retracing the stages of numeracy that I've described so far, whole civilizations have switched their perspective from numbers *describing* things, to numbers *explaining* things, *predicting* things, and even mystically *controlling* things.

This brings us to our fifth stage, the one we live in now. While the idea of numbers controlling our destiny may have begun as superstition, I suggest it's now a reality. For in our world today, numbers dominate. They figure in our daily lives and influence our decision-making right up to the level of global policy. We have come to rely on them and trust their significance in a way that would have been unimaginable even a few hundred years ago.

Numbers represent accuracy and precision. They are predictable and universal, which leads us to believe that they are entirely objective and unbiased. With sufficient numbers, *anything* can be described and precisely defined to whatever level the technology of the day allows. The moment humanity realized this, we set out to acquire knowledge through *measurement*. The appreciation and application of this principle led to a complete rethinking of what constitutes valuable *information*.

Once upon a time, and for many thousands of years, information consisted of stories, rituals, oral histories, and popular wisdom. This knowledge framed our personal and societal values, and decisions were made based on timeless human values. In our technological society today, information is mainly facts and figures; dates and amounts; statistics and specifications. If something cannot be measured and proven, then it has no validity in our era of rational thought. This has framed a different kind of value – the number-based value – that has, in turn, changed how we live of our lives. (These values will be introduced more formally later in this chapter.)

There is no doubt that the power and influence of numbers has improved our lives. This shift to empirical scientific principles is credited with the giant leaps in technology and progress of the last century. We have gained more knowledge and understanding in the last 250 years than in the preceding 25,000 years.

Meanwhile, that which cannot be measured has fallen to the wayside. Around the world, cultural values, spiritual beliefs, traditional knowledge, skills, and ancient customs have all been in decline. I believe we dismiss the unquantifiable at our peril. Those customs, values, and knowledge have existed since our earliest mammalian ancestor taught its young offspring a useful survival skill. They sustained us through millennia of existence without scientific textbooks or mathematical proofs. Yet today we leave them further behind, placing the majority of our trust in the rational, the scientific, and the measurable.

> *When you can measure what you are speaking about, and*
> *express it in numbers, you know something about it; but*
> *when you cannot measure it, when you cannot express it in*
> *numbers, your knowledge is of a meager and unsatisfactory*
> *kind: it may be the beginning of knowledge, but you have*
> *scarcely, in your thoughts, advanced to the stage of science,*
> *what ever the matter may be.*
> *– Lord Kelvin, physicist (1824–1907)*

The Power of Numbers

So why have numbers ascended to such a powerful position in our lives? The answer lies in three very potent properties of numbers themselves, which are crucial to understanding the causative factors behind our present predicament:

1. **Numbers are *limitless* (unending, infinite).** This significant, because it is a unique attribute. Numbers are the only thing we know to be entirely without end.

2. **Numbers are *linear* (a single scale going up or down).** Pick any two numbers, and one will always be greater than the other. One cannot say the same of other descriptors such as "happy" or "triangular".

3. **Numbers are *consistent* (across time, space, and culture).** Fifteen will always be greater than ten, and always by the same amount. The same mathematical operations will produce precisely the same results, no matter where, when, or by whom they are done.

I mentioned earlier that the properties of numbers endow them with an apparent objectivity. However, the power of numbers, like any other power, is not immune to misuse, abuse, or misrepresentation.

For example, it is not uncommon in our society to adjust numbers so that they "sound better" or work towards a particular goal. If I gave you two different measurements for the height of Mount Everest – 29,000 feet or 29,002 feet – which would you assume is more accurate? Quite likely, it would be the latter because it is more *precise*. So it happened that in 1852, surveyors used the best technology of the day to measure Mount Everest from six different locations, with the intention of reporting the average of all six measurements as the official height. That calculation produced a result of exactly 29,000 feet. However, the number looked too much like a rough estimate, so they altered their published figure to 29,002, a less accurate but seemingly more precise number.

It's easy to achieve this *precision effect* – putting in a few decimal places is often all it takes to boost apparent credibility. While the Mount Everest example is fairly benign, the world is rife with cases in which numbers have been selectively reported or enhanced to convey a certain perspective. Numbers need the proper context in order to have real validity; they cannot be trusted on their own. Alter the context and you alter their objectivity.

> Numbers are extremely powerful, but without context, they have no meaning in a qualitative human value system.

27

Good science is very particular about trying to provide full context for numbers, but the use of numbers is not limited to good science. Indeed, numbers can be used to 'prove' almost anything. Most people are familiar with the saying that there are three kinds of lies: "lies, damned lies, and statistics". The phrase describes three levels of falsehood: stating something that is not true, doing so with conscious intent to mislead, and using numbers to prove the false statement to be true. There is an old joke that "61% of all statistics are made up on the spot", but with numbers one doesn't have to resort to complete fabrication to obscure the reality, as evidenced by a few simple examples:

Say you have been encouraged to join a new workplace by being told that the average salary is $110 per hour. This sounds fantastic, until you discover that you are joining the four employees who earn $20 per hour, while the one manager makes $470 per hour.

$$\frac{20 + 20 + 20 + 20 + 470}{5} = 110$$

I have no idea what the number one cause of death among children in schools is, but do you think we should be trying to prevent it? One thing I can say with certainty is that no matter how much money is thrown at the 'problem', there will *always* be a number one cause of death among school children, just as there is one among hairdressers, drivers, and people who belong to lawn bowling clubs. *Ordinal* numbers (first, second, third, etc.) are often used to falsely convey importance.

Suppose you suffer from serious back pain. The doctor offers you a medication that only has a 50% chance of relieving the pain entirely, but one side effect is to triple your chance of developing pancreatic cancer. Would you take it? It might help to know that for your population, the general chance of pancreatic cancer is 0.002%. So, for a one-in-two chance of being completely pain-free, you are moving your risk to 0.006%. Does that change your answer?

I just read a newspaper article asserting that most sharks are benign to us and we are 15 times more likely to perish from having a coconut falling on our head. What does this mean? Is it just that there are 15 times more coconut-related deaths than those from sharks worldwide? How many people swim with sharks versus walk under palm trees? Does this include loss of limbs to sharks or just deaths? Are these comparative statistics equally applicable for people who live on the shores of North America?

Imagine a graduate school that over the last two years received the same number of applications from males as females (300 each), but 90% of the male applicants were accepted, while only 63% of the females got in. Contrast that with a school where, for each of the past two years, a higher proportion of females was accepted than males. The catch is that these are the *same* school and *same* years! Check out the table below to see for yourself how this can happen.

	Males accepted / applied	Females accepted / applied
Year 1	260 / 280 = 93%	50 / 50 = **100%**
Year 2	10 / 20 = 50%	140 / 250 = **59%**
Years 1 & 2 combined	270 / 300 = **90%**	190 / 300 = 63%

This quirk of sample size combinations is known as the Yule-Simpson effect (or Simpson's paradox), and was actually demonstrated in a refutation of a gender-bias lawsuit brought against the University of California, Berkeley in 1973.

For any situation, there is an infinite number of things to measure, each telling a different story. Select the right measurements, and we can argue any story we like.

> *Torture numbers, and they'll confess to anything.*
> *– Gregg Easterbrook, American writer*

Six years ago, I was attending a gathering of an environmental awareness group, listening to speakers share insights on some current issues. At the end of one talk, when the floor was opened up for questions, an

29

audience member stood up and asked if any of the guest experts could tell him how to distinguish good science from bad science. Like everyone else there, he was concerned about the health of the planet and of his community, but he was trying to sort out which side in the global warming debate was right. "Are we on the verge of a major man-made climate change or not?" No one could provide a satisfactory answer.

The mistake we make is to relegate that particular question to the realm of numbers in the first place. If we as a society are going to rely only on an inexact science to tell us how to act, then the decisions will be governed by whichever numbers happen to be more popular. Numbers can be used to confirm whatever you want, and for every set of numbers 'proving' man-made climate change, there can be presented another set to contradict it. Relying on numbers to determine our actions in such instances will result in arguments, indecision, and no action. Scientific fact should never be our *only* barometer of truth and value. Science provides data – it does not set the values by which that data should be interpreted.

This book is about the value that we place on numbers (like statistics and other measurements), and about values that are measured by numbers (like wealth and productivity). These two concepts must not be confused, but they are related: By assigning power to numbers in general, as has happened in the later stages of numeracy, it follows that we tend to have a greater respect for *number-based value systems* – our next topic of exploration.

Number-Based Value Systems

A *number-based value system* is one in which values are exclusively measured by numeric quantity. The best example of a number-based value system is *money*. Being number-based, the monetary value system shares the same three notable characteristics as numbers themselves: It is limitless, linear, and consistent. So, there is no limit to the value that money can represent; five dollars will always be worth more than two; and given the same input data, calculations of profit will produce the same results regardless of the culture or time in which the math is done.

Another number-based value system, one that is detailed in Chapter Nine, is *democracy* – decision-making by majority rule. Under a democratic system, ideas and possible actions are valued strictly based on the number of votes they receive. As with dollars, this system states that any quantifiable 'more' is always worth more: The choice that gets more votes is always more valuable, regardless of who is voting or why.

To demonstrate the influence of number-based values in our lives, the following chart contrasts them with human values and gives common examples of both. Which values do you think are more highly valued in our world today? Which of the examples seem "must-have" vs. "nice-to-have"?

	Number-based Value Systems	Human Value Systems
Properties	Measured by number Theoretically limitless More is always better Consistent & universal	Relative, subjective Cannot be measured by numbers Limited; can have enough Self-regulating
Examples	Personal wealth Economic growth Time, in terms of productivity Democratic voting	Happiness Justice Physiological needs Culture Spirituality

The unique properties of number-based value systems have made them very attractive to leaders and lay people alike. Numbers have acquired an unassailable 'super-human' power and precedence. The Age of Science and now the Digital Age have given us tremendous advances in technology and understanding, simply by providing us with the ability to precisely measure and then accurately create or reproduce things in the world around us. Given these gains, we now bestow numbers with a high value and level of respect. We believe in them to such an extent that we dismiss or downgrade other forms of thinking and evaluation –

those non-numeric intuitive processes that have guided our evolution for thousands of years.

A critical observation is that *none* of the three properties of numbers is present in any natural human system. At first blush, one might argue that our most basic physiological needs might have a quantitative basis. Certain chemical reactions need to take place in order for each one of us to survive – surely biochemistry has mathematical roots. However, the processes used to manage human physiology can hardly be said to be limitless, linear, or consistent. Even the most basic of human needs is relative. Put a person in an atmosphere of 100% pure oxygen and their hypothalamus kicks into overdrive, releasing a massive flood of neurotransmitters and hormones into the bloodstream which interfere with the heart's ability to pump blood and deliver that oxygen. More of a good thing is not always better. There is nothing limitless about the amount of food we can eat or the resources required to grow it. No one can accurately quantify emotional states, and there are no two emotions for which one is always more valuable than the other. What is important to a person one day, may be totally irrelevant the next. Human values, like natural systems, are relative and have boundaries.

> *Number-based value systems* are **limitless**,
> **linear**, and **consistent**, while innate human
> value systems have none of those properties.

The new scientific assertion is simple: "If you can't measure it, it doesn't exist." However, when we apply that kind of thinking to human values, such as happiness, culture, ethics, justice, progress, and wisdom – things that are intrinsically impossible to quantify – their importance can be dangerously diminished. This raises some interesting questions:

- What happens if our natural value systems are pushed aside in favour of numerical ones?

- Are number-based value systems really objective? Can they be trusted?

- What happens when we try to combine qualitative and
  quantitative value scales?

All of these questions will be explored in the chapters to come.

In Summary

Some level of numeracy has been associated with animals since our earliest evolution, and it is thus likely to be a natural and useful tool for our survival. Numbers themselves began their time with us as simple adjectives: a way of describing and comparing the quantity of things around us. With greater knowledge and ability came a growing need for higher *conceivable maximums* and more sophisticated numerical abilities, both of which eventually exceeded the grasp of most of us.

It is relevant to note that the first stage of numeracy, the *innate* stage, has limits. Only the first few numbers seem to be hard-wired into animal brains, and the natural ability to compare large quantities only works at ratios of about 1:2 or higher. This is consistent with the natural order of things – everything in nature has limits and boundaries. Contrast that with our learned level of numeracy – the level of limitless numbers and boundless mathematics.

Our natural thought processes do not use numbers, and important properties of mathematics still elude our instinctive comprehension. At the same time, we bestow upon them a powerful reverence, which is easily leveraged, such that numbers can be used to validate almost any position. Numeracy has come to exemplify the ultimate in precision and objective fact, and has altered our decision-making systems and values in significant ways. Numbers have come to do more than describe the things in our world; they now determine what we do with those things.

Human value systems are undoubtedly a complex field of study. While their operations and interpretations may not be clear or univer-sally agreed upon, one distinction that is very well-defined is their *qualitative* nature. This contrasts sharply with the *quantitative* nature of number-based value systems, which have no built-in concepts of "enough" or "too much" – concepts that are critical to the regulation and sustainability of any natural system.

Numbers may epitomize objectivity, but it must therefore follow that they are in no way biased towards the preservation of our species. As we will discover in later chapters of this book, the consequences can be disastrous when we hold values based on numbers higher than our own natural values.

> *I like mathematics because it is not human and has nothing particular to do with this planet or with the whole accidental universe - because, like Spinoza's God, it won't love us in return. – Bertrand Russell, philosopher (1872–1970)*

Chapter Two

Decision-making and Numbers

A good decision is based on knowledge and not on numbers.
– Plato, ancient Greek philosopher

S O, YOU DECIDED TO BUY this book. Have you ever thought about why you choose to do the things you do, what drives your decisions (especially financial ones), and how you evaluate outcomes? While numbers may play a big part in such processes, your subconscious brain is almost certainly not behaving the way you might expect it to. As for me, I hadn't given the issue much thought until an incident happened that was so seemingly irrational, it inspired the creation of the book you are now holding in your hands.

It was during one of those major life transitions. I had just moved into a new house in a new community and was in the process of selling the old house, the first property I had ever owned. Over the preceding ten years, I had put a lot of effort into that place. It was in a desirable location, on a quiet street just north of Toronto's well-known Danforth Avenue. The exposed side got a lot of light, and the kitchen opened out onto a deep and shady backyard.

Since I was selling the property privately, I spent a good deal of time driving back and forth into the city to facilitate the sale. In time, a buyer was found, and the agreement of purchase and sale was completed. The only remaining condition was a home inspection. Not surprisingly, when the inspector's report came back, it showed a number of items that might need attention. Many of these were trivial and inconsequential – things to be expected in an 80-year-old home. Still, the estimate to fix these items totalled $10,000, or about 2% of the purchase price. After faxing over the report, the buyer called and asked me what I wanted to do about it. Eager to see the sale completed, I suggested that we split the difference and take $5000 off the original offer. The buyer agreed and the deal was closed. I was happy and relieved to have it all behind me.

As I drove back to my new house, I wondered whether or not I had done the right thing. Relatively speaking, I had only gone down by 1% of the purchase price. That didn't seem so bad. Still, $5000 is a lot of money. As I pondered this, I noticed that my car was getting low on gas. I was just about to pull into a service station when I saw the price: 77.9 cents per litre. Surely I could do better than that, I thought, as I switched off my turning indicator and continued down the highway. A little further on, I filled up at 74.9 cents per litre, very pleased with my decision. Confidence in my financial acumen had been restored.

In one sense, my two transactions that day could not have been more different. The total cost of the gas was less than $40, so I might have saved about $1.50 – hardly comparable to the $5000 reduction on the house price. And yet I was struck by a curious realization: My pleasure at getting a deal on the gas fully alleviated the disappointment I had felt in making the concession on the sale. How could this be? How could I emotionally perceive a very small gain as balancing out a much larger loss?

One might suppose that in relative terms I had made a 4% gain at the pumps while only suffering a 1% drop in the house price. Thus, the valuations *within* each transaction resulted in emotional reactions that felt more or less equivalent. This makes some sense, but I still found it difficult to rationally consider the transactions as separate. The money still comes and goes from the same pocket, from the same limited bank account. It seemed that my feelings were unexpectedly out of step with the mathematical reality – so much so that this incident inspired me to dig deeper. What was going on?

The Value(s) of a Dollar

When it comes to understanding how we value monetary transactions, the first challenge is that the word "value" has at least two different meanings. Consider the different 'values' of a hockey ticket: Its retail price is an impersonal measure of value, but what you're willing to pay for that ticket is not. The latter is a measure of something different: the deeply personal value of how strongly you desire something. For this reason, economists use the term *"utility"* instead of *"value"* to describe the satisfaction received from a transaction. *Utility* is their way of attempting to translate between money's number-based value system, and the less quantifiable world of human desires and emotions.

While the *monetary value* of each dollar is the same for everyone (every dollar is valued at exactly 100 cents), the *utility* of each dollar is not. The difference is explained by the concept of *marginal value* or *marginal utility* – the idea that the satisfaction we receive from any item depends on how many we already have. If you are shopping for apples, you are much more likely to care about getting a second apple if you only have one, than you would be about adding one more apple to a bag of 100. The *law of diminishing marginal utility* states that as we acquire more of anything (be it apples or dollars), the satisfaction derived from each additional unit goes down. A dollar to a homeless person has a far higher marginal utility than it would to a corporate executive, because their personal net worth valuations are different.

It is fairly simple to grasp that the utility of a dollar will be different for people at different income levels. Most people would accept the central tenet of *marginal utility theory* – that our net worth (the total amount of money we have) determines the utility of each dollar we earn or spend. You may also agree with what economists call the *rational-agent model* – the idea that humans act in a rational manner. However, if all your transactions were guided by an entirely rational, number-based value system, then the utility (satisfaction) of each financial transaction would be relative to a single base-line value: your net worth, and nothing else.

If this conclusion seems a bit foreign to you, you're not alone. The premise does not describe the reality of most people's lives – we simply don't think that way. If you are living well above the poverty line, a dollar-off coupon should be almost meaningless to you, regardless of the product. However, if you are like most people, your desire for getting a deal takes precedence over any calculated value of the deal relative to your net worth. According to *marginal utility theory*, each of my dollars should have carried the same weight, and the small savings at the gas pump should never have felt equal to the monetary loss on my house. And yet it did.

This shows up a very serious limitation of classic economic theory: It simply does not explain the *emotional value* we put on things. Our innate value systems are not based on numbers, and our brains are not wired to calculate numerically. No matter how much economists attempt to refine mathematical formulas to explain human behaviour, it does not change the fact that we do not always behave as rational, wealth-maximizing entities. So the question continues: What drives our financial decision-making, if not rational numerical calculations?

Prospect Theory: A More Human Explanation

To say that human behaviour is not always rational does not mean that it's entirely unpredictable. Collectively, we can exhibit remarkably predictive behaviours, as any successful advertising executive will tell you. In the quest to understand how we make our everyday choices, behavioural economists and psychologists have been studying common numerically 'irrational' habits. Here are two examples of what they've learned which provide clues to our mathematically surprising choices:

> Most people would willingly walk a few blocks to a discount store to buy a book for $7 that cost $21 in a closer store. Few people would do the same to save $14 on a $2000 laptop computer sold at the same establishments. The distance and the $14 saving are rationally the same for both cases, however they are emotionally different, based on the overall transaction value.

> When offered the choice between a guaranteed $100 gain or a 50% chance at a $250 gain, the majority of people choose the first option – a *risk-averse* choice – even though the mathematics puts the value of the second choice higher at $125. However, when offered the choice between a guaranteed $100 loss or a 50% chance of a $250 loss, the majority of people choose the second option – a *risk-seeking* choice – even though that choice is numerically costlier.

In 1979, a proposal known as *prospect theory* was put forward by Daniel Kahneman and Amos Tversky to try and explain the above observations. In its simplest terms, the theory states that people faced with deciding amongst alternatives will first set a 'neutral' *reference point* for themselves. Options on one side of the reference point are considered gains, while those on the other side are considered losses. Probabilities and values of potential outcomes are then evaluated to determine the best course of action. For financial decisions, people will take action based on the expected savings or monetary gain of that particular choice. They do not consider the impact of each decision on their absolute net worth.

Prospect theory introduces three important new factors in our mental calculations of maximizing satisfaction. The first is that *where we set the neutral reference point* will strongly influence the outcome. To illustrate this, imagine that you have purchased a non-refundable movie ticket, but then are invited to do something more desirable in the same time slot. Objectively, the choice is quite clear: (a) attend the movie, or (b) do something you would prefer to do. In both cases, the ticket price is already spent (known in economic terms as a *sunk cost*), so mathematically it should have no influence on the choice. But it does. If you are like most people, you will feel an obligation to not 'waste' the ticket. This is a case in which the reference point is set in the *past*. You are down the price of the ticket, so you attend the movie to balance out the 'loss'. However, if your reference point is set in the *present*, then the ticket cost is already gone and no longer a factor, so you will accept the invitation to do something more enjoyable.

The second factor is that *the options on the two sides of the reference point are not evaluated equivalently*. The theory proposes that we all share a consistent trait for loss aversion, which skews our calculations. Studies suggest that losses are psychologically twice as powerful as gains. A $30 loss is therefore emotionally equivalent to a $60 gain. This helps explain why we would choose a 50% chance of avoiding a $250 loss over taking a guaranteed $100 loss. Humans tend to be risk-averse for gains but risk-seeking for losses.

The third factor is our *diminishing sensitivity* to changes in both gains and losses as they move further out from the reference point.

Starting with the money we have now as our reference point, our subjective distinction between the $7 and $21 book prices would be much more profound than our distinction between the $2000 and $2014 laptop prices.

We can now apply some prospect theory to my own story. My reference point for the house sale could have been my current bank balance, which was about to go up substantially, or my minimum selling price, which was still exceeded by the final agreement. Thus, I perceived the $5000 adjustment to be a small reduction to a gain, not a loss. Had I been asked to give back $5000 after I'd been paid the full price of the house, my innate loss aversion would have kicked in and I would not so easily have accepted the compromise. The magnitude of the sale would also have diminished my sensitivity to the change in value. In contrast, the first gas station exceeded my mental reference point for the price of gas. By driving to the next station, I avoided a 'loss' and produced a gain – one that felt substantial for the purchase.

Keep in mind that a pure *number-based value system* has a single bottom line – in this case, my net worth. Under such a value system, a tiny gain at the gas pumps should never have eradicated the loss on the house sale. In reality, I was not focused on changes to my absolute net worth. My brain was focused on the monetary changes within each transaction – changes that were much more relative. The power of the prospect theory is that it helps to explain actual human behaviour in economic situations – behaviour that is not constrained to mathematical rationality.

The Value in the Errors of our Ways

In recent experiments at Yale University, capuchin monkeys have been shown to make exactly the same financial 'errors' as humans. Scientists created a culture of money amongst their subjects, giving them small metal tokens which could be used to buy food and treats. They then subjected the monkeys to transactions designed to replicate market characteristics such as bargains, gambles, etc. Sure enough, the primates demonstrated the same numerically-irrational behaviours as humans, seeking 'deals' and avoiding 'losses' in ways that make no mathematical sense. Since capuchin monkeys deviated from our ancestral line about 35 million years ago, researchers suggest that these common traits are physiologically wired into our brains.

We are only beginning to understand our innate decision-making mechanisms and the roles that they may have played in our phenomenal success as a species. A lot of the most surprising research results have just been accumulated in the last few decades, and some of the best work was done by Kahneman, who received a Nobel prize in Economics for his contributions. Consider the following scenario, which provides a snapshot of some of the *cognitive biases* and non-mathematical influences that we apply to our decisions.

You have just rented a high-end mountain bike for a two-month trek through South America. The dealer offers you an optional insurance policy against theft of the bike. If you do not pay the $50 premium, you will be responsible for the full $2000 cost of replacing the bike if it gets stolen. Since a different rental agency offered you the same insurance policy at $65 the day before, you think $50 is a good price. If you accept the $50 policy on that basis, you are exhibiting an *anchoring bias,* allowing the higher premium to influence your decision instead of the true value of the insurance. (We all do this when we buy things just because they are "on sale".)

Let's say your tour guide had assured you that 99% of his clients have never had any problem with bike theft. This wording introduces a *framing bias* which might lead you to skip the insurance. Had you been told that 1% of bicycles are stolen, that framing might lead you down a different path. Indeed, humans are often susceptible to *overweighting* unlikely events, so you might start to focus on what would happen if your bike was stolen. If you had recently heard other stories of theft in the area, an *availability bias* would further magnify your perceived likelihood that this same thing would happen to you.

A mathematician would use probability to calculate the rational value of the insurance at $20 ($2000 x 1%). By this calculation, you would be paying a $50 premium for an insurance policy with a theoretical value of $20. If you were thinking like a mathematician, with your present state as your reference point, you would almost certainly refuse the insurance. However, if you're a cautious pessimist, you might set your reference point at the worst case scenario. In doing so, you fixate on what would happen if a theft did occur, and you compare the $2000 to the $50 premium that would cover the loss. Therefore, you would perceive the net value to be $1950. Furthermore, you may wish to avoid the very human emotion of *regret*. You would soon forget about paying a $50 premium, but it would take a long time to forgive yourself for losing an uninsured bike.

In his book <u>Thinking, Fast and Slow</u>, Kahneman presents these biases as undesirable flaws – traps that cause us to behave irrationally, especially when making number-based decisions. Conscious efforts to eliminate such cognitive biases are the foundation of scientific enquiry and improvement. Indeed, our spectacular advances in knowledge and technology would not be possible without rational, fact-based method-ology. However, one cannot dismiss the very real benefits associated with some of our 'flawed' decision-making. For instance, the peace of mind offered by an insurance policy, even an overpriced one, is real, as is the pain of regret. When we measure the outcomes by human values, even a mathematically irrational decision may prove to be in our best interest.

Value System Selection

For every decision we make, our ultimate choice is determined by the value system we choose to employ. There is a big difference between using numbers in making decisions (i.e. being rational) and making decisions based on number-based values (e.g. maximizing wealth). By way of example, here are three ways that people might decide upon a travel method for a family vacation:

> Anne chooses to take the car because she is frightened by the perceived dangers of aircraft mishaps. She just heard about a commuter plane that went down in some Asian country and is convinced that travel by car will be safer.

> Brian has calculated that by driving the family to another airport in a nearby city he can get cheap airline tickets with a deep discount carrier. By leaving very early in the morning he can also save the cost of an overnight stay.

Carol knows that air travel is safer than most other options. Even so, she ultimately decides that train tickets, while not the cheapest option, are still within her budget and would give the kids lots to look at while she and her partner relax.

Anne demonstrates the concept of making decisions in the absence of true facts. Most humans are inept at guessing and processing statistical risk and probability. We have irrational fears of highly improbable events, and even as a society we spend inordinate sums to counteract negligible dangers while ignoring more common and prevalent ones.

Brian is not ignoring the facts. He has worked hard to research his options, and he evaluates them using the number-based value of money alone. He is working under the assumption that the best vacation choices will be the ones that minimize his costs – no matter what the sacrifice to convenience and comfort.

Carol has also done her research and has a tight budget. The difference is that once she has determined the affordable options, she makes her final decision based on human values. She might just as easily have rejected air travel because of its high carbon footprint. The point is that she is not ignoring the objective facts, but she is not limiting her evaluation to financial concerns either.

The distinction I'm making can be subtle. Let's consider a larger example: If a government makes a decision to promote marriage and family values, it makes sense for policy-makers to look at the statistics on marriage and divorce rates. They might even consider financial tax incentives for married citizens. The point is that such numbers and financial policies are simply the means to an end, and the end values at stake are human ones: promoting marriage and family. Policies to grow the economy, on the other hand, might use similar means, but the ultimate values being promoted (such as increased wealth) are number-based, which puts such policies into a different class.

One useful rule-of-thumb for distinguishing these two kinds of thinking is to ask whether or not the objective is bounded by a limit. There's a limit to how many citizens can get married, but it's theoretically possible to grow an economy to any imaginable number. Hence, economic growth is a number-based value. Similarly, there is a limit to how much added enjoyment Carol and her family can gain by taking the train – it is a human value and will not always be the better choice.

In light of the enormous benefits that civilization has received from science, economic prosperity, and other rational, number-driven behaviours, why should we ever question the use of number-based values? How could our mathematically-flawed innate values ever serve us better? To answer these questions, let us turn to a fascinating activity called "The Ultimatum Game".

This classic experiment works with two unrelated subjects. The first person is offered $100 on the condition that it is split, in whatever amount they choose, with the second person. If the second person agrees to the proportions of the split, the subjects are paid accordingly and the game is over. If they do not agree, then no one gets anything. According to basic economic sense, the second player should never reject a proposed split. Why not take any amount of money, regardless of what the first person gets? Within a number-based value system, every possible non-zero division of the $100 is a win-win situation for both parties. And yet consistently, with subjects across the whole spectrum of cultural and socio-economic conditions, most splits were between 40% and 50%, and most offers that were less than 30% were rejected. These results may come as no surprise to you – if you were offered $20 by the other person while they kept $80, you might well have rejected the deal too. However, such rejections totally contradict any assumption that humans are rational, self-interested creatures who consistently seek to maximize their wealth.

The Ultimatum Game reveals an important operation of our human value system: a sense of fair play. In a society created around collaborative behaviours, it's easy to see why the value of fairness would be critical to the flourishing of progress, and why, for the good of the community, those who exhibit anti-social greed would be slapped for it.

Prospect theory and the Ultimatum Game don't necessarily contradict the suggestion that we always act in our best self-interest – perhaps we do. But what they clearly demonstrate is that non-numerical values can exert a greater influence on choices than a desire for wealth. It is quite likely that evolution has favoured our loss aversion, collaborative tendencies, and sense of fairness as being more important than numerically coming out ahead.

Species Dominance and Survival

The fact that you and I are able to consider these questions is convincing evidence that these built-in values have conveyed a survival advantage – our species is still around. Since those values determined every action and reaction of our ancient ancestors, nature had plenty of opportunity to evaluate their efficacy and decide which value systems would survive and be passed on. Despite their numerically irrational quirks, evolution has clearly found our innate values to be more than acceptable.

Indeed, these values are essential to our continued prominence as a species. As an obvious example, having children has a significantly negative financial impact on parents (at least in the developed world), and yet people greatly value starting families. Similarly, there's nothing mathematically rational about giving money to charity or volunteering one's time. The whole concept of collaboration and personal sacrifice only works when individuals are willing to look beyond their personal gain and work towards a greater good. Such behaviours convey a huge advantage and lead to progress. But when progress begins to be measured by number-based values instead, the benefits tend to be shorter-lived, and there is evidence as old as our species to prove it.

Thousands of years ago, the earliest *Homo sapiens* learned that by hunting in groups, it was possible to bring down a huge bison or mammoth. Such big game could provide a source of food, tools, and warmth for a long time. Then we got too smart for our own good. If one kill provided significant utility, then surely killing more would provide many times as much. In one of our earliest examples of efficiency run amok, our Upper Palaeolithic ancestors figured out how to drive massive herds of game over cliffs. Small bands of hunters were able to slaughter thousands of animals, most of which were left to rot. While nature's bounty could withstand this onslaught for a time, plenty of species were hunted to extinction (especially on islands such as New Zealand and Madagascar). Suddenly the application of progress based on utility maximization had just the opposite effect, reducing utility to zero.

Thousands of years later, we still apply exactly the same techno-logical thinking to our resource management. We sweep the seas clean of fish stocks or find better ways to pull oil out of the ground or clear rainforests to raise beef cattle – all with dramatic but short-lived benefits. In the last century, the science of the Green Revolution more than doubled agricultural output in developing nations. We are only now experiencing the impact of the other shoe falling: vulnerable monocultures, accumulated pesticides, and exhausted land that no longer grows anything. There is no question that number-based values are the present de facto standard of our society. It seems that progress has advanced but important lessons have not been learned.

If we accept that our innate, non-numeric value systems have played an important role in our continued presence on the planet, when did we start consistently making choices that run counter to those values – and why do we continue to do so? I suspect that the shift coincides with the beginning of agriculture. When humans began to 'own' resources, trade goods, and plan for the future, such practices called for the evolution of numeracy and numeric values. The rise of civilization over the last 10,000 years has been characterized by an increasing prevalence of number-based value systems, in which outcomes are quantified and more is always better. While such thinking almost always provides immediate and significant short-term benefits, over the long-term it has also led to unsustainable growth, violent conflict, envir-onmental challenges, empire collapse, and even species extinctions.

The time lag between spectacular pay-offs and catastrophic conse-quences is a major factor in our inability to fully appreciate the dangers of allowing number-based values to rule our decisions. I propose that the three ground-breaking factors of *prospect theory* can explain why we persist in this paradigm and can help us to see some of its dangers.

1 Neutral reference point

Prospect theory says we evaluate decision options from a *neutral refer-ence point*, dividing them into losses and gains accordingly. Some of the most damaging costs of number-based value thinking only become apparent after multiple generations have gone by. At that point, the reference point will inevitably have shifted. We don't intuitively appreciate the decline in fish stocks or the devastating loss of forest cover because none of us were around to see what the planet looked like a hundred or more years ago. Similarly, as our standard of living increases, our reference point moves along with it. We no longer appreciate our gains as gains – they've become the new normal, and any return to earlier values is seen as a loss.

2 Loss aversion

To forego the short-term benefits of number-based values, we would have to take a stand and believe that our sacrifice now will pay off in the long run. Unfortunately, our instinctive bias to *loss aversion* would be working against this kind of thinking. When faced with the possibility of loss, we are willing to take a risk. But when faced with potential gains, we are risk-averse. So if building a nuclear power plant means that we can make a profit and produce energy now, we are more likely to do so because it is a sure gain. Risk of environmental disaster and dealing with spent fuel exists only in an unseen future. On the flip side, paying more on our hydro bills for investment in renewable energy can be considered a short-term loss. Psychologically, such losses are twice as powerful as gains, especially when those gains may only be realized some years down the road.

3 Declining sensitivity

The *law of diminishing marginal utility* says that as we acquire more of anything, the satisfaction derived from each additional unit goes down. Every dollar added to our bank balance gives us less satisfaction than the one before it. Therefore, while it is true that the affluence of society is on the rise, it takes ever-increasing amounts of money to give us equivalent joy. This phenomenon is more generally stated by the *declining sensitivity* factor of prospect theory. As we become more affluent, we are more likely to take what we have for granted, and changes to our standard of living have to move in ever-greater leaps in order for us to be truly impressed. Our current generation of children take fantastic advances in mobile phone technology for granted. It takes much more to exceed their expectations than it would have for their parents or grandparents.

> Prospect theory can be used to identify three dangers of number-based values: a moving reference point, short-term loss aversion, and a declining sensitivity to affluence.

Personal Preferences for Number-Based Values

And so it is that number-based value systems are now a dominant driver of societal decisions. This would not be possible without each of us also adopting numbers-based values at a personal level. The growing awareness of our brain's biological ineptitude with math has not diminished our reverence for numbers; on the contrary, we actually strive to have numbers play a more prominent role in our decision-making, while suppressing our innate subjective values.

There are several possible reasons for this. For one, decisions using number-based values are generally easier to implement. Many of life's options can be distilled down to easily compared numbers, resulting in choices that we believe to be objective and outside the realm of human foibles and individual peculiarities. Removing our personal values from decisions has other advantages as well – especially when you consider that the demand for decision-making is greater than ever before. From career options to mobile phones to the supermarket aisle, there has been a phenomenal rise in the number of choices we must make in our lives. The common belief is that increased choice leads to more satisfaction and greater happiness. But research is now showing that greater choice has exactly the opposite effect: When our choices extend beyond what is truly important (in terms of our core values), the incidence of *post-choice regret* goes up, regardless of the choice made. This *paradox of choice* can trigger stress and disappointment – in a sense, we manufacture regret for whichever option was left behind. By relying on the objectivity of numbers to make the choice we distance ourselves from the decision, reducing the potential for such regret. Numbers are rational, and so we put our faith in them to make decisions that are clearly justifiable.

For similar reasons, number-based value decisions are also easier to defend. When we set aside our innate, natural mechanisms for making value judgements and resort to more objectively rationalized mathematical mechanisms, we relinquish much of our human responsibility for the actions we take. We are no longer justifying a personal choice; the numbers made the choice for us. In essence, we make the whole process 'safer' by not having to defend our choices based solely on personal principles or preferences. Instead, we can hide behind whichever numbers we selected as inputs. This is illustrated in present-day politics: Most contentious policy decisions are backed up by a host of budget numbers or statistics, disguising a preferred policy as an inevitable consequence of numbers.

> Decisions using number-based values are easy to make, easy to defend, and seemingly less susceptible to our innate numerical irrationalities.

I am not immune to this thinking myself. I abhor making arbitrary choices and feel the need to rationalize nearly every decision that I make, sometimes by manufacturing reasons for choosing one option over another. When I buy laundry detergent, I don't default to a familiar brand. I apply some basic values on environmental friendliness, and then spend a few minutes calculating the best dollar value. Even at vending machines, I'm often ambivalent about the brand of snack, but I might base my selection on the net weight of the products. While this may seem strange, it relieves me of the burden of making a suboptimal or 'wrong' choice. Of course, 'right' and 'wrong' are defined by the value system we choose to apply. Pretzels might be the right gram-per-dollar choice, but would be wrong for a chocolate-lover. Unfortunately, by applying number-based values to more easily determine what is 'right', I lessen my awareness of what my personal preferences are for things – those which are right by different value scales.

> The more we suppress our own value systems, the less familiar we will be with exactly what they are.

We can eventually get to a point where, if we try to ignore the numbers and just focus on what we want or believe to be important, we discover that we don't really know what that is anymore. I recall dating a woman who always seemed to have an excellent idea of what she wanted. When we got together, she knew what she wanted to do, where she wanted to eat, and what she would order. I was happy to go along with whatever her choices were. One day she asked me to make more of the decisions, and I soon realized I had no clue what my preferences were. I suspect that exercising my choices more might have helped me to refine them.

The same is true of society today. As we allow our lives, our communities, our nations, and the globe to be shaped by number-based values, we lose touch with powerful human values that still matter. Despite our inability to instinctively make good numeric decisions, a huge proportion of the planet now measures success by number and numeric wealth. It is how we manage our lives, it is the basis of most of our interactions, and it is how we run our countries and indeed our planet. Is there a connection between this pervasive trend and the crises looming on the horizon? I believe there is, and that is what I have set out to uncover in the chapters that follow.

> *It's not hard to make decisions when you know what your values are. – Roy Disney (film writer, producer, nephew of Walt Disney)*

In Summary

A key premise of economic theory is that we are all rational, *utility-maximizing* entities, who balance costs and benefits to determine how we will spend our time and money in the precise manner that gives us maximum satisfaction. While it makes sense that we would seek what is best for ourselves, mathematics cannot always predict or explain what we deem to be in our best self-interest. The sheer magnitude of the discrepancy between the rational math and my emotional reactions on the day I sold my house finally brought that to my attention. There were so many more factors at work: My disappointment in accepting a cut in the house price was tempered by my relief that the sale was completed; the ubiquitous frustration at having to stop and fill the gas tank was offset by getting a better price per litre. Such emotional inputs cannot be quantified, but they have an obvious and profound impact on our resulting state of happiness.

The *law of diminishing marginal utility* is interesting because it implies limits to the satisfaction that can be derived from having more of something, but it only works within a human value system. Numeric values are consistent and limitless; they do not diminish with quantity. If you own four shovels, the fifth shovel provides negligible utility, but if you sell shovels, each one can be sold at full value. Hence, within a purely number-based value system, such as you might find in a commercial business, the law of diminishing marginal utility does not apply. More is always better.

It is easy for us as individuals to get sucked into the same paradigm of more always being better, but our built-in values rarely follow that rule. The result can be seemingly irrational human behaviour, as described by prospect theory and our innate cognitive biases. The problem comes when we consistently treat such behaviours as flaws, to be avoided by consciously relying on numbers instead. As a proponent of math and science, I'm certainly not advocating a dismissal of numeric facts and measurements. But using numbers in decision-making does not require outcomes to be weighed using number-based values. This is a vital distinction. There are often sound evolutionary reasons why we make certain choices at the expense of numerically maximized returns, as demonstrated by The Ultimatum Game.

Furthermore, if the goal of individuals and humanity as a whole is truly to maximize satisfaction, then *satisfaction* is what must be used to evaluate our options and human decisions. Objectively measuring our success by numbers is inappropriate to that goal – more (of anything!) does not necessarily produce more satisfaction.

Even so, our society has a strong tendency to default to the monetary value scale – our most pervasive number-based value system – for more and more decisions. It is ubiquitous, simple to use, and produces choices that are readily and 'objectively' rationalized to others. Consider the power we attribute to money. We devote an overwhelming amount of time and energy to acquiring it, and it is the predominant yardstick by which we measure our world and everything in it, including our success. It impacts every aspect of our daily lives and determines the actions of governments the world over. Economic growth has become the undisputed quest of human endeavour – a Sisyphean task on a hill that has no summit. Where do the *other* human values fit in to all this?

Values such as health, justice, relationships, freedom, and culture have been with us for millions of years. Generally speaking, we don't gain money by volunteering in our communities, celebrating religious holidays, appreciating art, going to the doctor when we are sick, or having children. How did we become a species that, despite these examples and countless others, makes most of its collective decisions using the single, relatively new value of financial wealth?

Thousands of years ago, our ancestors strived to maximize utility and ended up wiping out entire species on a variety of islands. Today, the planet is our island, and we have no where else to go. Any belief that we no longer make such mistakes is simply ignoring the evidence to the contrary: Number-based values and the resulting destructive actions are more prevalent now than ever before. They are seductively powerful, but when we give them precedence over human values and then rig the outcome by using only numeric values to measure our success, we're dangerously relinquishing the determination of our future to numbers.

Instead of blindly assuming that our lot is continually improving, we must learn to measure the success or failure of an ever-growing global economy with more than just monetary valuations. Either we choose to live differently, or we let the planet's finite resources make that decision for us.

> *Everything that can be counted does not necessarily count;*
> *everything that counts cannot necessarily be counted.*
> *– Albert Einstein*

Chapter Three

Money – The Number Culture

The chief value of money lies in the fact that one lives in a
world in which it is overestimated. – Henry Louis Mencken,
American journalist/critic (1880–1956)

IN 1993, I TRAVELED TO Nepal for an expedition with the Australian
School of Mountaineering. It was my first visit to the "developing"
world and in many ways that trip changed my life. As we left the teem-
ing chaos of Kathmandu and trekked towards our first climbing peak in
the Annapurna region, it became apparent that the rules of commerce
were different out there. For the first few nights, we stayed in teahouses
where an honour system prevailed. We were expected to tally our own
food and drink orders, calculate what we owed, and pay up before we
departed. It was a level of trust that enhanced the experience.

Further along, we began to encounter trailside souvenir stalls –
usually little more than a board spanning some rocks – with trinkets
ranging from ubiquitous tourist T-shirts to unique handcrafted padlocks.
Of course there were no prices; we were expected to haggle. At first, I
was reticent to engage the vendors. Haggling over goods and prices is
an art form in many countries, and I had no experience with the nuances
of marketplace negotiation. Finally, in a beautiful hillside village, I
decided to take the plunge. I bargained with vendors for a Tibetan
Mahākāla mask, a vest, and some other items. At the end of the
process, I felt that we had all gotten a fair price.

Fast forward a decade to a communal lunch at an experiential
education conference in Boulder, Colorado. I was proudly wearing the
Nepalese vest, my favourite accessory, when the woman across from
me asked where I had got it. I told her about my trip to the Himalayas

and how much fun we had negotiating with the local sellers for some souvenirs. I was completely taken aback when she voiced an indignant disapproval of my conduct:

"I think that is offensive! When we travel in poorer countries, we always pay whatever price the vendor asks for. How dare you come into their homeland – you with all your North American wealth – and haggle over a few rupees with those people. The differences are mere pennies to you, but have significant worth to them! How could you be so insensitive?"

I was immediately embarrassed by the accusation, but I soon realized that she had brought to light a serious conundrum: What is the fair and correct thing for a foreign visitor to do? Pay the first price quoted? Pay what you would back home? Pay what the locals pay? Or haggle for the going tourist rate? Although some people are quite clear on which side they stand, the ethics of this dilemma are not so simple.

This chapter explores the whole issue of money and values within transactions, and the inconsistencies revealed when they cross borders. In order to gain a more complete understanding of the concepts and what's at stake, we will begin at the very beginning… with the history of money itself.

A Brief History of Money

If the behaviour of chimpanzees is any indication of our evolutionary past, our earliest form of currency was simple reciprocity – or what I like to call an *indebtedness of favours*. If one of their peers share food or help with acts of grooming, chimpanzees tend to remember the kindness and repay the 'debt' with complementary favours over time. This behaviour has been observed in other animals as well, indicating that as social creatures, we innately keep a tally of favours received, paying back what we 'owe' with reciprocal acts of kindness. It is easy to imagine that such reciprocity results in communal harmony and species survival. While the favours returned may not be the same as the ones received, a relative balance is maintained.

This concept of reciprocity works best within a community of pre-existing relationships. When a transaction took place between strangers, it was more commonly by *barter*. Exploring barter is a good way to grasp the later role of money. In its earliest forms, individuals and groups would trade objects or services that they valued less (perhaps having plenty of them) for those that they valued more. Anyone participating in a trade was doing so on the presumption that a desire was being satisfied – that their net value was going up, so to speak – by making the exchange. Since the same principle would be operating on both sides of the exchange, both sides were gaining. Consider two ancient ancestors, I'll call them Fred and Gail. Fred makes arrowheads and Gail makes baskets. If Fred exchanges one of his arrowheads for one of Gail's baskets, then we can say that a basket is worth more (or the same) to Fred than an arrowhead, since he chose to trade one for the other. A similar statement can be made for Gail. Thus, barter is based on non-mathematical principles: Both sides swap goods, and suddenly both sides are 'worth' more.

The challenging downside of barter is that it relies on the *dual coincidence of wants*: It requires a person with object A looking for object B to meet a person who has object B and happens to be looking for object A at the same time. In other words, if Fred wants a basket and only has an arrowhead to trade, he needs to find someone who has a basket and is willing to trade it for an arrowhead.

The easiest solution to this challenge was to insert a third item that was generally recognized as being of value to everyone. Hence the emergence of some early forms of money: rice, livestock, eggs, and salt, all once used as currencies. Thus, our first money took the form of tangible items which could be used directly by the recipient. Even if Gail didn't happen to need rice at that moment, she could still accept it from Fred in exchange for a basket, knowing that she could trade that rice for something that she did want at a later time.

Eventually it became apparent that *anything* could be used as money so long as people recognized it as representing some value. Usable items like rice were replaced with representative objects of wealth like beads, precious stones, and other decorative items. The practical value of metals soon led to the first coins in about 700 BC. When the weight and security of metal coins became problematic, people began storing excess coins in central locations, for which they received a printed paper receipt. Since such paper could be exchanged in return for the coins, it held the equivalent value, and society had its first paper currency beginning with the Chinese over 1000 years ago. The concept of printed money as an I-owe-you (IOU) note still holds true. Indeed banknotes from the Bank of England still say that the Chief Cashier "promise[s] to pay the bearer on demand the sum of…" – showing the historical roots of settling the debt in precious metal.

Though we still have paper currency and coins today, we are rapidly shifting away from physical representations of money. As of 2013, the *gold standard*, linking money's value to metal, is gone. Bank balances are now numbers in a database, not cash in a vault. Automatic payroll deposits, electronic transfers, and debit or credit card transactions are nothing more than slight changes to databases. Money has thus evolved from objects of real *tangible* value (e.g. rice), to objects of *representative* value (e.g. coins), to a *conceptual memory* of wealth (numbers in a bank database).

Our money is now an understanding of universal acceptance based on total trust. If I buy groceries by credit card, for example, the local supermarket gives me my food based on a *belief* that when my credit card numbers go into their computer and it chats briefly with some database, then there is sufficient evidence that managers of a financial institution somewhere in the world believe that when their computer requests a payment from my bank account database, the electronic balance will be sufficient to cover my credit card bill – those funds being the result of a belief my employer had that I brought value to his workplace when my salary was automatically deposited by digital transfer. Phew!

> Money has evolved from an *object* you needed for survival, to a *currency* that might buy what you needed for survival, to a *number in a database* that you need to trust for survival.

This evolution is very important. Money is now just a number – the epitome of a number-based value system. And yet our interactions with it are primarily to satisfy our many and varied non-numerical concepts of value: food, shelter, transportation, entertainment, etc. We might refer to these as *absolute values*, because they are intrinsic to us as humans and not innately measured by number. Curiously, the true value of money has evolved in two entirely contradictory directions:

- As its convenience and universal acceptance have grown, the value of money has increased tremendously. That value is based not only on the *quantity* of goods and services that can be exchanged for it, but also on the limitless *diversity* of those goods and services. "Everything has a price." You can apply money to just about anything around the globe, meaning that the power and potential value of money is immense.

- Money has evolved from things you could use directly for your survival (a high value in the human hierarchy of priorities) to an intrinsic value of nothing. Rice and eggs could be eaten, and even coins could theoretically be melted down to make arrowheads or pots. However, an electronic bank balance, in the absence of all of the supporting infrastructures and commercial trust systems, is worth nothing. The *absolute value* of digital money is zilch.

> *Only after the last tree has been cut down… the last river has been poisoned… the last fish caught, only then will you find that money cannot be eaten. – Cree Prophesy*

Putting a Price on Value

Going back to barter for a moment, trading an arrowhead for a basket might suggest that the value of the two objects is equal, but that's misleading: Each value is relative to the individual. We can't even conclude that the *utility* of the basket to Fred equals the utility of the arrowhead to Gail. All we know is that both parties are getting an object which is worth more (or the same) to them as the object that they are giving. This has an interesting effect. Assuming that both parties are fully informed and willing participants, then *every trade is a fair trade* – a win-win situation that increases utility on both sides.

There is no math in barter exchanges. It's only when you introduce the concept of money that numbers are required, and the effects of that are significant. Let's consider the effect on our arrowhead/basket trans-action when a new entity, bead money, slips into the middle. Assume that Fred and Gail agree on four beads for her basket. This tells us two things: The basket is worth four beads *or more* to Fred, and the basket is worth four beads *or less* to Gail. Note that the values are still relative to individuals, and not necessarily equal. Perhaps the basket is worth six beads to Fred but only three beads to Gail. A difference in relative values is fine for pure barter, but when money is introduced into trans-actions, there can be no ambiguous inequalities. The arithmetic is simple and specific, and all transactions must follow mathematical laws. The value of every good and service must be calculated into a specific *price*.

So how do we set that price? How do we put a number on value? The question is more complex than you might imagine. You have now been introduced to at least two kinds of value: *marginal* and *absolute*. *Marginal value* is how much we are willing to pay for an object in the marketplace, based on the quantity that we already have. *Absolute value* is the concept of how strongly we desire an object, based on our personal needs. The marginal value (cost) of an ounce of gold on the global market is several times that of an egg-laying chicken. However, in the absence of a market in which to trade that gold for food, the chicken would have a much higher absolute value – you can't eat gold! Similarly, air has a high absolute value (we all need it to live), but a low marginal value (it is so common that we don't pay for it). How-ever, if we were in outer space, its marginal value – what we'd be willing to pay for it – would be astronomically higher. (Note that while it is absolute value that truly matters, it's not possible to measure that value with numbers – to do so would require the introduction of a marketplace, and then you would be measuring marginal value!)

Money and a marketplace make it possible to measure *marginal value* with ease. But even within the marketplace, additional concepts can further complicate matters when it comes to setting a price. For example, a seller may consider the emotional value attached to an object, or how much it cost to acquire the object and make a profit. If the object is available from other sellers, there might be a *going rate* (*market value*) set by the market itself. Unfortunately, the system only allows for a single value of money to be exchanged – which is it to be?

? What it's really worth to the buyer (absolute value)
? What it's really worth to the seller (absolute value)
? What the buyer is willing to pay (marginal value)
? What the seller is willing to sell for (marginal value)
? The cost to the seller (with or without a profit)
? The going market rate (market value)
? The price that is finally agreed to and paid

The answer to this complex question is what economics is all about. In the end, the last definition is often the most important one, since it is the final result and cannot be disputed. If we accept that the true monetary value of an object or service is the negotiated amount that was ultimately paid for it, then money does more than just settle the bill – it actually has to be exchanged in order to positively determine that object's value. A good example of this is in real estate: The monetary value of a house is not the asking price – it's the closing price.

The marketplace has evolved to be very good at resolving this final valuation, but there are still limitations and assumptions. A relatively level playing field must exist and extraneous human values must be excluded from the equations. For instance, if parents are selling the family home to their daughter, the price paid on paper might not be the true monetary value of the house, despite our definition. Similarly, if someone is unduly coerced into buying or selling something, the price might be arbitrarily higher or lower than would otherwise be the case. For values to be valid, there must be sufficient freedom for transactions to take place across the full marketplace.

Ultimately, market valuations are based on what a buyer is willing to pay and what a seller is willing to take. There are a few ways to determine a price, based on the culture you are looking at. In North American stores, the seller typically sets the final price – take it or leave it. In Nepal, sellers use a more traditional way to determine price: it is negotiated with every buyer.

We're now closer to resolving the dilemma that opened this chapter. Since, haggling in a Nepalese marketplace is how they set their prices, engaging in the practice is not intrinsically wrong. However, we still need to consider that I had a completely different valuation for the currency than did my Nepalese vendor. To understand the effects of this, let's take a look at how value crosses international and cultural borders.

Money and the Global Economy

Money was originally developed to bridge gaps of time and distance – to store wealth from the time it was acquired until when it was needed, or to easily move it from one place to another. In the history of civilization, the introduction of money happens independently at different points for different societies, suggesting it to be an almost inevitable outcome of social evolution. There were exceptions: A few sophisticated societies survived quite well with no creation of money to represent value. The commerce of the Incas was based on exchange of goods and/or labour. Even their enormous wealth of gold was never used as the basis of a monetary system, although it was clearly valued as a material itself. Such exceptions not withstanding, there is little doubt that the simplicity and universality of mathematical principles have allowed monetary systems to become the keystone of commerce, and thereby economics.

In the early days of international and cross-cultural trade, even commercial enterprises that were money-based at home often had to return to barter in order to trade goods abroad, since the value (and representations) of money were not equally recognized on both sides. Spices were exchanged for precious stones, beaver pelts for pots and pans, and both sides came out ahead. Just as it was for individuals, this kind of global bartering was generally beneficial to both trading partners. Each side was usually getting something that they did not have access to any other way, such as products based on uniquely available resources, or localized skills and quality.

Since mathematics easily crosses linguistic, political, and cultural boundaries, it wasn't long before monetary systems became ubiquitous and internationally linked. Once that happened, countries could trade more than unique goods and territorial resources: They could also trade common goods, competing on price and leveraging regional cost advantages. For example, both Europe and North America had trees, but the size of the forests in the New World conveyed a huge commercial advantage for industries there, such as boat building. In 1776, Adam Smith, , the father of modern economics, wrote:

> *It is the maxim of every prudent master of a family,*
> *never to attempt to make at home what it will cost him*
> *more to make than to buy...What is prudence in the*
> *conduct of every private family, can scarce be folly in*
> *that of a great kingdom. If a foreign country can*
> *supply us with a commodity cheaper than we ourselves*
> *can make it, better buy it of them with some part of the*
> *produce of our own industry, employed in a way in*
> *which we have some advantage.*
> *– The Wealth of Nations (Book IV, Chapter II)*

This made excellent economic sense in Smith's time, and is still a successful strategy today (when success is measured by numbers). However, as price increasingly becomes the sole decision-making factor for sourcing goods, we have to ask *why* the commodity is cheaper from the foreign country. If this is due to a natural advantage, that's one thing. But what if lower prices are the result of other practices that go against values in the consuming country, such as child or slave labour?

Smith's maxim is a perfect example of a monetary value system taking undeserved precedence over human value systems. He seems to be suggesting that financial cost be our exclusive measure of wisdom. Why is the cheapest solution necessarily the most prudent? Why must local production, which honours the values of learning, entrepreneurial spirit, pride, experience, investment, craftsmanship, skill diversity, and other sources of human joy and accomplishment, be pushed aside so that the mathematics of profit reign supreme? Yet there is no question that a few powerful nations took advantage of the math, and the world soon divided into 'have' and 'have-not' countries.

As developing economies struggled to catch up, the predominant incentive for trade gradually changed from leveraging natural or cultural advantages to leveraging disparities of wealth and standards of living. This is where we find ourselves today. Labour and resource costs are substantially lower in the poorer countries where the products are made, than in the richer countries where the products are ultimately sold. The difference far exceeds the cost of shipping huge quantities of goods vast distances, so the work is done abroad, in a practice called *outsourcing*.

> *Simon & Schuster, the book publisher, [...] would ship its*
> *books over to India and pay Indians $50 a month*
> *(compared to $1,000 a month in the United States)*
> *to type them by hand into computers...*
> *– Thomas L. Friedman, <u>The World is Flat</u>*

The success of this strategy relies on the unique properties of the monetary value system on which the practice is based. The math, as always, is the first to jump the gaps because it instantly makes equivalent sense from one economy to the next. Five dollars plus five dollars equals ten dollars, no matter where you are on the planet. The big difference, of course, is what that ten dollars can buy. If you own a global business, a single dollar paid out to a foreign worker can represent a very different level of buying power than one paid to a domestic worker. If a labour-dollar has a much higher value abroad, then you can spend less and get similar results. If you are then selling your product in the domestic market where a single dollar has a lower value (relative to the cost of living), your revenue will be based on purchase-dollars, and the price of the product will be much higher. The critical point to the company and its shareholders is that a dollar is a dollar – spent abroad or charged at home. If you can produce goods at a tenth of the cost, you can charge half the original price, sell more units, and make substantially more profit on each one.

> *Outsourcing and globalization of manufacturing allows*
> *companies to reduce costs, benefits consumers with lower*
> *cost goods and services, causes economic expansion that*
> *reduces unemployment, and increases productivity and*
> *job creation. – Larry Elder, talk-show host*

Many economists and commercial interests contend that globalization is a win/win opportunity for everyone. Countries at the top of the heap are spending less for goods, and developing countries are growing their economies. There are two problems with this argument: Firstly, it rigs the outcome by using only monetary values to measure its success, while ignoring all other effects. The full reality is that too many human values are crushed in its wake. Secondly, even within the number-based values, the claimed success of globalization is a mathematical half-truth. If every hour I get a dollar and you get a dime, then I can claim that we're both getting richer, but in fact you are getting comparatively poorer.

> Globalization and outsourcing are not just exploitations of economic gaps. They are profit at the expense of other value systems.

While western countries may pride themselves on progressive environmental or labour policies, they are readily buying goods from developing countries that may have totally unacceptable practices. Product safety and child labour laws vary from country to country, but with global markets, unsafe or child-made products cross international boundaries all the time. There are manufacturers who still make a business decision of whether or not to save money by using lead-based paint in making toys for children. The use of these paints has continued with alarming frequency in the last few years, despite the known health hazards. The thinking works both ways: Canada continues to export asbestos products that are banned as unsafe at home. These and many other disturbing practices clearly highlight a conflict between long-term human values and short-term monetary ones – a conflict that is not limited to global transactions, by the way.

We are now living in a global economic explosion – a *flattening* of the world (as author Thomas Friedman puts it in The World is Flat) – unlike any in the history of the planet. Friedman's term is referring to market access. Today's technology allows goods to be made anywhere, for any market; services can be performed anywhere on the globe, again for practically any market. Ore can be mined in Africa, processed in Europe, fashioned into parts in China using designs from North America, assembled in South America, and sold as finished goods in

Australia. Orders for American drive-ins can be taken by call centre operators in India. The playing field, according to Friedman, has been levelled as never before.

And yet, has it? True, the developing world now has competitive access to practically every market of the developed world's economies, but the major rewards of that competitive advantage are going into the pockets of corporations in the developed countries. Capitalist theory proposes that if this practice is continued, the wealth will slowly propagate, thereby eliminating the discrepancies. Cost-of-living and wage-expectation differences will eventually be levelled by market forces, as wealth flows from one economy to the other. Even if this were true, reducing the massive gap between rich and poor is unlikely to happen at the same exponential rate as the growth. The wealthy players, who hold a hugely disproportionate share of the power, will work hard to oppose this propagation and protect their outsourcing advantage. The players may now be on the same field, but it is not a *level* playing field – not yet and not by a long shot. U.S. President John F. Kennedy asserted that "A rising tide lifts all boats." But what if you are already in the water up to your neck and you don't own a boat?

Furthermore, the cost of labour is not the only thing that is different in the developing world. Cultural expectations, lifestyles, social benefits, population density, infrastructures, availability of products and services, values, *everything* is profoundly different. Yet even the most cherished attributes of these countries are subject to erosion in this global flattening – a flattening that is entirely dependent on the consistency and cultural indifference of money. Globalization reduces local resilience (as skills become more concentrated and specialized by region), consumes energy (as goods are unnecessarily transported around the world), defies autonomy (as local authorities become overwhelmed by the power of international conglomerates), exacerbates environmental concerns (as consumers live further away from the sites of resource degradation), discourages linguistic diversity (as English, the international language of commerce, becomes expected), and wipes out cultural diversity (as entertainment and social norms converge to the most powerful common denominators). Still, the expansion of global free trade continues apace.

The effects of globalization are not particularly new to civilization. We have already experienced them with the spread of the Roman Empire and the colonization of the New World, to name two obvious examples. But we are only now beginning to understand what happens when diversity flattens out on this planet: At best, entire cultures rise up in revolt; at worst, they simply disappear.

> *Culture is the collective programming of the human mind*
> *that distinguishes the members of one human group from*
> *those of another. Culture in this sense is a system of*
> *collectively held values. – Geert Hofstede, Dutch writer*

Speaking of cultural differences…

Back to Nepal

In light of global differences in the value of money, it becomes easier to understand the paradigm of the woman who sat across from me at that lunch table. From her perspective, I was exploiting the gaps between the Nepalese and the North American economies, thereby perpetuating my own wealth and the vendor's relative poverty, which she objected to. Similar objections have led to the creation of *fair trade* industries, such as those for coffee and native artwork. She was clearly and laudably championing the human values of fairness and equality.

In today's march towards an increasingly unrestricted global economy in which success tends to be measured by monetary scales alone, these values go largely ignored. Consider the less conscientious commercial importers, who buy goods in bulk from the developing world at minimal cost, and then sell them for a huge mark-up to wealthier countries. In a number-based value system, this strategy is considered smart. In a human-based value system, it is exploitation.

Upon reflection, my values seem to have been somewhere in between. By adopting the accepted practice of negotiating prices, I believed I was respecting the culture of the country I was in and their currency. I also had faith in the strength of the tourist trade and the haggling experience of the merchants. I think the attraction of haggling for both visiting and local consumers is similar to the attraction of buying something "on sale" in North America. The seller knows what they need to make a profit and the buyer feels like they're getting a deal. There were plenty of other shoppers, and I did not suspect for a second that a seller would accept an unfairly low price. Indeed, there is no doubt in my mind that the Nepalese vendors adjusted their starting prices much higher, based on the fact that I wasn't a local – and rightly so. While I wanted to feel that I was getting a deal, I assumed that the vendor was coming out ahead too. Ultimately, both my perspective and the one of the woman who challenged me have merit. That's the thing about human values like fairness – there are few easy answers.

The complicating factor is the consistency of the monetary value system. Money facilitates direct comparisons of value, but *which* value – marginal? absolute? Comparisons across widely differing economies don't always make sense. Moreover, the very fact that money stores wealth and can retain that value when moved between economies means that inconsistencies can be exploited. Even though my mutually agreed-upon price for Nepalese souvenirs was about as honest a transaction as you can get, the simple action of money crossing cultures made its fairness subject to question.

While barter might seem like a throwback to outdated market practices, it could have provided the perfect solution to my original marketplace dilemma. I conjecture that if I had traded, say, a nice wristwatch for my selected items, everyone would have been happy, including my highly moral colleague at the conference!

In Summary

We covered a lot of ground in this chapter, just to resolve a value dilemma in a little village market in South Asia. I hope the things that we learned along the way made it well worth the trip, as was the case with my original journey there.

We began with the history of money, and the almost inevitable social evolution that moved the practice of bartering into the international monetary system that we have today. It's easy to see why money became so attractive. First, it solved the *coincidence of needs* dilemma inherent in the barter system. Secondly, money allowed value to be stored, divided, combined, and easily carried from one transaction to the next.

However, once currency moved from items of *tangible* utility to items that only *represented* real value, its inherent value became based on trust (and an assumption that the other participant in any transaction shared the same belief in that value system). Money has now evolved to where it no longer has any intrinsic value at all. Without a belief in the banking system, a number in a database is absolutely worthless. Since we do have commercial trust systems in place, we commonly accept that money has value – and yet how long can we assume that those systems will remain intact, reliable, and uncompromised? As monetary systems grow in complexity and continue to move towards the ethereal realm of digital bits and bytes, they are subject to some interesting 'tinkering' – legal and otherwise. (We will discuss ways of altering this kind of value by math alone in Chapter Six.)

Over the last few hundred years, the universal properties of money have made it the accepted medium of international and cross-cultural trade. Initially such trade leveraged uniquely advantageous regional attributes. However, as the common value of money began to highlight wealth disparities, countries began competing on price alone. Since value must be translated into money in one environment (for example when a product is purchased in China) and then translated back in another (when the product is sold in North America), it's easy to exploit the value gaps to generate high profits and inflate consumption. There is a big difference between importing silk made in China using an artistry perfected over thousands of years, and importing 'native American' moccasins made in China because the labour and materials are cheap. The first celebrates cultural diversity, the second makes a farce of it.

The creation of a single planetary market has also resulted in more homogenous global cultures, with a loss of societal diversity. Even ideological boundaries (such as that between capitalism and socialism) were eventually porous (if not ultimately susceptible) to the sheer power of a universal monetary value system. While many economists claim that globalization is good for everyone, I remain sceptical. But win/win situations are not impossible – the original barter system proves that. In fact, the power of the internet is now being used in a practice called *swap trading* as an alternate solution to the challenge of the *dual coincidence of wants*. The chances of finding a compatible barter partner are much better when you can reach out to millions of people. Such practices not only bring back the original advantages of barter trading, they also put objects in the hands of people where they will have the highest utility. This reduces the number of items being thrown into landfill and frees up resources that would have gone into producing unneeded additional items – a win-win-win on all sides.

Of course, increasing utility, wasting less, and preserving resources are *absolute values,* and such objectives may not be supported by those who measure values numerically. Free market economists may choose to ignore the ethical problems, but the indifference of money will come back to haunt them. Money only has value in a marketplace. The true value of things cannot be determined by assigning them a number. If there is nothing left to buy, and no unspoiled space left, such financial success will be hollow indeed.

> *We no longer see the world as a single entity. We've moved*
> *to cities and we think the economy is what gives us our life,*
> *that if the economy is strong we can afford garbage*
> *collection and sewage disposal and fresh food and water*
> *and electricity. We go through life thinking that money is the*
> *key to having whatever we want, without regard to what it*
> *does to the rest of the world.*
> *– David Suzuki, Canadian environmentalist*

Chapter Four

What's Your Motivation?

*Classic economic theory, based as it is on an inadequate
theory of human motivation, could be revolutionized by
accepting the reality of higher human needs, including the
impulse to self actualization and the love for the highest
values. – Abraham Maslow, psychologist (1908–70)*

M Y FIRST PAID JOBS WERE teenage summer stints in research
and hospital laboratories, arranged for me by my father. I would
wash glassware or prepare Petri dishes, and spend as much time as I
could with the regular staff without getting in the way. I didn't take on
these assignments for the money; the primary motivation was meeting
the people, learning new things, and having something useful to do.
That being said, I was always thrilled at receiving a cheque at the end,
regardless of the amount – to me it was unimaginable wealth.

It wasn't until I was a co-op student at the University of Waterloo,
alternating four months in the classroom with four months at a real job,
that I encountered my first real job interviews. At the end of each inter-
view, the employer would invariably ask if I had any other questions.
When I said no, they would remind me that I hadn't asked about the
salary. It rarely failed to amaze them that I had no particular interest in
knowing what the salary was. The fact that I was to be paid was a given
– I assumed that my needs would be met. My real concerns were:
Where would I be posted? Would I enjoy the work? And would I be up
to the tasks?

Over the years, my attitude never changed. While the need to earn
money was a fact of life, I never considered changing jobs just to earn
a higher wage. I have even happily changed my career to one with a

lower salary when other personal considerations were more favourable. This does not make me better or worse than anyone else; it just makes me somewhat atypical. For whatever reason, I was never particularly attracted to consumerism. As a result, I rarely spent the money that I had. I fully appreciated the comforts that money could bring, and I was happy to earn it, but its prominence as a workplace motivator was just not that high on the list.

I should point out that I was not born independently wealthy, nor have I ever received a huge lottery win. I have the same basic needs as everyone else. While some might think that my attitude towards money puts me in the minority, there is in fact a lot of evidence to suggest that money might not be the motivator that we assume it to be. In this chapter, we take a closer look at human needs and motivations, exploring when money helps us towards our goals – and the point at which it ceases to be the answer.

Human Needs and Motivations

In the 1940s, the American psychologist Abraham Maslow created what is now a classic and widely accepted theory of human motivation. You may be familiar with his Hierarchy of Needs, which uses a pyramid model to describe five ascending levels, from physiological needs at the bottom to self-actualization at the top.

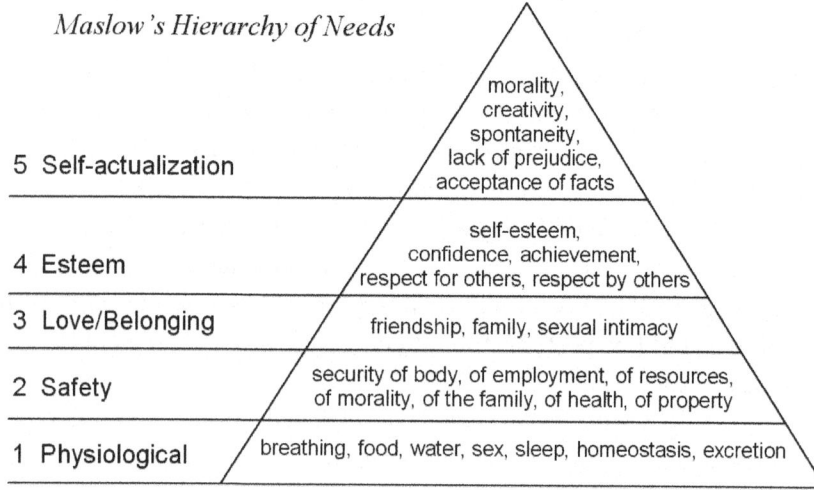

Maslow's Hierarchy of Needs

5 Self-actualization — morality, creativity, spontaneity, lack of prejudice, acceptance of facts

4 Esteem — self-esteem, confidence, achievement, respect for others, respect by others

3 Love/Belonging — friendship, family, sexual intimacy

2 Safety — security of body, of employment, of resources, of morality, of the family, of health, of property

1 Physiological — breathing, food, water, sex, sleep, homeostasis, excretion

Maslow's Hierarchy of Needs is a very useful framework for analyzing and understanding human behaviour and growth. According to this theory, we are innately motivated to move up the pyramid, level by level, and usually in sequence. Only when needs are satisfied at one level can we then focus on achieving the next one. The lower levels, which Maslow called *deficiency needs*, deal with the obvious needs of survival itself; thus, we are constantly motivated to ensure that they are met. When these deficiency needs are satisfied, however, *growth needs* compel us move to the top level in the hierarchy. Maslow called this an impulse towards *self-actualization* or personal growth.

Generally speaking, once you have moved past a level, those needs will no longer need to be prioritized. However, if a lower set of needs is unmet for an extended period of time, you will temporarily drop back down until those lower level needs are reasonably satisfied. So if, for example, your level 1 needs of food and sleep are not being met, you will be motivated to focus on those requirements. Friendships or security (levels 2 and 3) will tend to receive less attention, and self-esteem (level 4) may well be ignored. By the same token, you should not expect a co-worker to work effectively as a team member (level 3) when they're having their house re-possessed (level 2), and you can't reliably expect a salesperson to achieve their sales target (level 4) when they're dealing with a death in their family (level 3).

Of course, this description simplifies what is naturally a complex set of impulses. Most people's motivations at any time include elements of all of the drivers. *Self-actualizers* (people at level 5) are focused on personal growth, but are still motivated to eat and socialize. Similarly, a homeless person whose main focus is finding a meal (level 1) and shelter for the night (level 2) can still be concerned with social relationships (level 3), how their friends perceive them (level 4), and the meaning of life (level 5).

Given the fact that so much of our daily lives seems to be tied to financial concerns in one way or another, it is perhaps interesting to note that money and the pursuit of wealth *for its own sake* do not explicitly appear anywhere in the pyramid. The basic human needs described by Maslow's theory predate the concept of money. Our species survived millennia without money, and could theoretically do so again. Still, there is no denying that in our industrialized world, we need money to satisfy most lower level needs. "We have to pay the bills" is a common reality.

However, money's applicability has crept up the pyramid to the point where it is seen as potentially influential at every level. Money has evolved from being a *tool* to support the human need for survival to being a *thing of value* in and of itself, based on the belief that it is now necessary for satisfying all other needs. The danger in this belief is that it's not actually true. There are plenty of wealthy people who have not reached the upper half of the pyramid, and plenty of lower income people who have. Humans do not need money to be spontaneous, creative, or even happy.

> Money and wealth have acquired incredible stature as universal motivators, despite the fact that we have no *innate* need for money at all.

Yet in our society, many people living well above the poverty line pursue wealth under the false assumption that without it, they can never hope to have the leisure time to live a creative and meaningful life. It's a familiar trap, and an unfortunate by-product of our monetary value system. Needing money to pay for our survival needs, we enter a world of number-based values which has no limits and therefore no concept of "enough". We can easily become consumed by financial goals and worries, losing connection with the actual needs and values that we had hoped to 'buy' in the process. Studies suggest that, regardless of income level, the more people are *driven by a desire for wealth*, the poorer their psychological health on a range of measures. The distinguishing factor is not the amount of money that an individual has, but its place in their value system.

Once our survival needs are met, perspective is everything. When the need for money becomes disconnected from the needs that it is being used to satisfy, something changes. It's as if we switch over onto another track; one where the concept of enough is ignored. While it is tempting to characterize that as simple greed, such labels depend on the value system you are viewing from, and when numbers are involved, we are all susceptible to such accusations.

Are We Motivated by Greed?

It is common in business to think of salespeople as being very much driven by numbers to define their success. Much of my consulting career has relied on frequent collaborations with excellent salespeople, and these interactions have given me insights into how *value-by-numbers* can significantly influence a personal value system.

One highly motivated colleague comes to mind. He was passionate about his sales vocation, hard-working, curious, and dedicated, but what fascinated me most was that numbers seemed to rule his life at every level. He would diligently measure his sales performance at each stage: counting calls made, referrals acquired, proposals written, and hours put in. His success was almost exclusively measured on percentages and net revenue. If his income was down, he would put in more hours, even if it meant that everything else (relaxation, family, etc.) had to be whittled down or pushed aside. I suspect that his approach was not unique among the sales elite. Indeed, some in the profession have an unfortunate reputation for crossing ethical lines in their pursuit of higher numbers – think used cars, telemarketing, insurance, etc. The question is, once we are in a number-based value system like commission sales, are we more susceptible to being motivated by greed? Let's consider this for a moment.

To begin with, it makes sense that a numbers-driven value system begins with maximizing profit as the highest ideal, because success is measured on a linear scale: More profit is better. This makes it difficult to define greed *within* a number-based value system; after all, the idea of greed is associated with excess, and what is an *excessive* number? The more prosperous salespeople that I've worked with attribute their success to hard work or diligently-honed talent – both of which would qualify their income as well-earned. What's wrong with being motivated to succeed?

This brings up an interesting point. I had always thought that my aversion to measuring success by financial gain might preclude anyone thinking of me as greedy, but I was wrong. The perception of greed versus impartial fair-dealing depends entirely on what value system you are operating within. We often assume that the person sitting across from us shares our values. If you are driven by numbers, it makes perfect sense to assume that everyone else you deal with is also out to maximize their financial return. And so it happened once that the tables were turned on me. After working on a very lucrative contract, I told the salesperson I was not content with my established flat rate that we had applied to similar but smaller sales. My motivation for doing so was emotional; the arrangement didn't feel right. To his number-based frame of mind, this was a cash grab; an irrational and unfair desire for more. While I saw qualitative differences and expressed my feelings, he saw someone greedily questioning the objectivity of the numbers. Perceptions of greed work in both directions.

Greed is therefore not the black and white, good vs. evil scenario that we like to think it is. Nor is it a core human motivator. It is simply the term that individuals apply to highly-motivated others whose measures of success are different from theirs, whether they be based on numbers or emotions.

Salary and (Dis)Satisfaction

No matter which value system you tend to operate within, one cannot ignore the near-necessity of money to fulfill Maslow's lower level needs in modern society. For centuries, employers have recognized the obvious incentive of money for labour, and considered salary to be a very simple and effective motivational tool. If you want to increase the motivation of your workers, you simply increase the salary, right? If only it were that easy! Research, theory, and real-life experience are showing this question to be much more nuanced than you might think.

Fourteen years after Maslow published his pyramid, another American psychologist, Frederick Herzberg, conducted studies to determine which factors in an employee's work environment motivated them. From his conclusions, he divided the factors into two categories: those that determined *satisfaction* and those that determined *dissatisfaction*. These are shown in a table on the next page.

Factors Affecting Job Attitudes

Leading to Satisfaction	Leading to Dissatisfaction
<ul><li>Achievement</li><li>Recognition</li><li>Work itself</li><li>Responsibility</li><li>Advancement</li><li>Personal growth</li></ul>	<ul><li>Company policy</li><li>Supervision</li><li>Relationship with boss</li><li>Work conditions</li><li>Salary</li><li>Job security</li><li>Relationship with peers</li></ul>

The key to understanding Herzberg's theory is that the satisfiers and dissatisfiers are not opposites. In other words, if you remove all of the factors which cause dissatisfaction, you do not get satisfaction; you just get a lack of dissatisfaction. Accordingly, Herzberg labelled the factors on the left the *true motivators* and those on the right the *hygiene factors*.

Herzberg's distinction between satisfaction and a lack of dissatisfaction may seem subtle, but it provides a pivotal insight into the factors affecting job attitudes and productivity. If a factory worker is labouring in a sweltering hot, dimly lit room, one can reduce some of the worker's dissatisfaction by adding air conditioning and better lighting, but those factors do not actually motivate the worker. In other words, once those environmental problems have been removed, one can't make the person more productive by adding even more air conditioners and lighting. This limitation is what makes working conditions a *hygiene factor* and not a *motivator*.

It is interesting to note that Herzberg found salary to be a *hygiene factor*. If a worker's salary is too low, then you can raise their wage in order to remove that particular source of dissatisfaction. However, his research concluded that there is a point at which the cause and effect will have been dealt with. If workers are already making a decent salary, giving them more will not motivate them to do better work. Since money is commonly believed to be a strong motivator in the workplace, this is a striking result.

Motivations can be generally divided into two categories: *extrinsic* (external factors such as tangible rewards or punishment), and *intrinsic* (internal drivers such as achieving a personal goal or having fun). Note that these correlate strongly with Herzberg's *hygiene factors* (mostly extrinsic) and *true motivators* (mostly intrinsic). Research has found that intrinsic motivation is much more powerful than extrinsic motivation, but if both are combined for the same task, there is a curious effect: The extrinsic motivation can actually displace the intrinsic motivation in what is called the *overjustification effect*. For instance, even if we love our job, when we are paid to do it, the salary assumes a greater importance than our natural joy in the work.

It is therefore no coincidence that labour strife consistently revolves around salary, job security, company policy, supervision, and work conditions – i.e. *hygiene factors* – the determinants of dissatisfaction. Since the advent of the Industrial Revolution, sufficiently dissatisfied employees have organized labour unions – an action which, speaking from my own experience, has the potential for permanently altering the nature of human interactions in an organization. It is not just that the union/management relationship is often adversarial. Unionization also shifts the value discussions so that they take place exclusively in the realm of numbers, and away from the true motivators that require more individualized implementation.

In effect, collective agreements keep us embroiled in *hygiene factors*, which do not make us more productive, nor do they bring us greater satisfaction. How does this happen? Firstly, they rely almost exclusively on numbers and complex formulas in an attempt to equitably define individual worth, group benefits, and workplace policies, resulting in inflexible systems that are vulnerable to manipulation. Secondly, they fail to address the real *motivators* that generate true employee satisfaction – motivators which are unquantifiable human values, and therefore cannot be measured. The larger the company, the greater the tendency to focus on more easily measured, negotiated, and adjusted hygiene factors such as salary, work conditions, job security formulas, leave policy, and supervision ratios. Qualitative motivators like achievement, recognition, and personal growth do not respond well to one-size-fits-all strategies. Once again, numbers win the day.

This is notable given that unions were originally created to protect humanity from overzealous and abusive applications of the number-based value system. The social and environmental conditions during the Industrial Revolution, which would be considered intolerable by today's standards, were the result of a familiar push to generate enormous profits, using technology and power at the expense of workers and habitat. Employers focused on the numbers instead of the people, and now their labour counterparts seem to do the same. This is not an argument for or against unions; it's simply another example of how conflicts can arise within a number-based value system, and how their resolutions are limited by that same system.

If Herzberg is right, the power of addressing hygiene factors like salary is limited to only eliminating dissatisfaction. This is not to say that money provides no motivational value at all. In 2007, scientists at the University of Bonn conducted a series of experiments that showed fascinating outcomes on what motivates us. In the research, subjects were given tasks to solve while brain scanning instruments measured the activity in their ventral striatum. This region of the brain (called the *reward system*) is activated when an individual has "an experience worth aspiring to." When subjects completed their task correctly, blood flow to the ventral striatum increased. When they got it wrong, it decreased. Getting the task right was a proven motivation.

The interesting part came with some variations to the experiment. When a financial reward was added for correctly completed tasks, ventral striatum activity increased relative to the size of the reward, suggesting that money was indeed a motivation. However, when the experiment was conducted in pairs, with different reward amounts for the two participants (a difference that both were aware of), a surprising result was noted. Even when both subjects got the task right, only the individual receiving the higher reward showed positive motivation activity. The one who received less than his partner did not show the usual response to being rewarded – instead his blood flow *dropped*. His reward was no longer rewarding if someone else received more.

It seems that the financial gain was significantly overshadowed by the de-motivating influence of a perceived lack of fairness or a sense of competitiveness. (It might be notable that the experiment subjects were all men.) Despite the fact that the lesser-rewarded person was still gaining money, he was actually made *less* happy by the payment. Even when the experiments were conducted with no monetary rewards, activation for test subjects who got the task right was at its highest when their co-player got it wrong. Clearly, the comparison of one person's achievement or reward with another's was more important than the satisfaction of a right answer or even a monetary gain.

The Bonn experiments demonstrate that money can be a motivator, but the relationship is complex. When money becomes just a salary – what everyone else is getting – even a high one will not necessarily result in greater satisfaction. In fact, one study at the Southern Methodist University with 188 female university students showed that when rewards do not reflect competence, higher rewards lead to *less* intrinsic motivation. When rewards do reflect competence, higher rewards lead to *greater* intrinsic motivation. So when our salary level is not attached to the human values of achievement and recognition for a job well done, it becomes just another hygiene factor. Unfortunately, this hygiene factor can become the main thing that we focus upon – often at the expense of our personal satisfaction.

> *One should guard against preaching to young people*
> *success in the customary form as the main aim in life. The*
> *most important motive for work in school and in life is*
> *pleasure in work, pleasure in its result, and the knowledge of*
> *the value of the result to the community. – Albert Einstein*

Wealth and The Pursuit of Happiness

The great business statistician W. Edwards Deming told a wonderfully ironic story of how he once asked a group of people if they were actually motivated by money. After some reflection, they all said that just having more money would not make them truly happier, but they unanimously volunteered to participate in lengthy trials to gather more data on the question! Everyone is happy to receive more money. But does having more money make us happier? (There is a difference!)

One powerful attraction of the monetary value system is its ability to inspire a pervasive sense of optimism. Regardless of our personal net worth, we can always envision the potential for our fortune to improve.

Because the essence of our financial wealth is simply a number, we're well aware that it can always be increased, no matter how much (or how little) we already have. The potential to be rich, no matter how unlikely, always exists. It hangs in our collective imagination like a dangling carrot.

We have all heard about people who have struck it rich through lotteries, the stock market, or even criminal activity. Despite the low odds of gaining wealth from these gambles, we optimistically pursue them, partly because money, if acquired, can break down so many other barriers in life. You may come from the wrong side of the tracks, your ancestry might be an embattled minority in your community, you might even have physical challenges that put you at a disadvantage; but if you can acquire enough money, all of that can be overcome. Even those who break the law arguably get very different treatment in the justice system depending on how much money they can devote to their defence. Financial wealth is something that everybody understands. More than any other value, money can cross barriers of class systems, racial discrimination, and cultural differences. Wealth cannot be ignored.

> The monetary value system's definition
> of success is uniquely unconditional.
> Wealth confers irrefutable power,
> easily measured and easily wielded.

This can make the monetary value system very attractive to those who seek greater happiness, even if they have all the necessities of life. The promise, of course, is that more money will bring more happiness. On a rational level, we know that this is not necessarily true. But one glance at a lottery kiosk line-up on a high jackpot night will show you that it's a powerful and pervasive hope, just the same.

So how does this desire for wealth mesh with our actual human needs and motivations? If we apply the concept of *hygiene factors* to Maslow's lower level needs such as food, we can see that there are natural limitations to the satisfaction that money can buy. If a person is hungry, they can be 'motivated' by food only until they have eaten their fill. After that need is satisfied, the body does not crave food – it has had enough, and will in fact reject excessive amounts.

> There is a limit to satisfying primary human needs. Once the need has been satisfied, excess quantities do not produce additional benefit.

Herzberg's research has shown that there are similar limitations to the benefits of a salary. However, we might not easily recognize salary as a *hygiene factor* because that critical feedback mechanism of "sufficiency" is missing from the monetary value system. It is always possible to have more money. Indeed, when there is enough to raise the standard of living, humans adapt quite quickly to such changes – especially when everyone around them is experiencing a similar improvement. This process, called *hedonic adaptation*, changes our baseline expectations. Unlike hunger, the desire for more money does not tend to go away.

> *Money never made a man happy yet, nor will it.*
> *There is nothing in its nature to produce happiness.*
> *The more a man has, the more he wants. Instead of*
> *filling a vacuum, it makes one. If it satisfies one want,*
> *it doubles and trebles that want another way.*
> *– Benjamin Franklin, polymath (1706-1790)*

Where human need and excess money do intersect is in the area of security: Even prehistoric man knew that once he had eaten his fill, it was well worth gathering and storing more food against leaner times ahead. The presence of such food caches would not be a great indicator of an individual's happiness at any given moment, but having them raised that individual's prospects for surviving a long winter. Saving wealth endows a similar sense of security, and money has a long shelf life.

But does money make us happy? Attempts to answer this question are problematic. For example, many people enjoy spending money *and* saving it, and also derive pleasure from giving it away. Yet each of the three outcomes is in contradiction to the other two. So what is the value we are pursuing? (We explore more of this particular three-sided paradox in Chapter Ten.)

Similarly, what do we mean by "happy"? At Princeton, Daniel Kahneman analyzed survey results obtained in the USA, comparing income to *life evaluation* and *emotional well-being*. *Life evaluation* rated a person's impression of how good their life was, on a scale from 0 to 10, while *emotional well-being* measured how happy they were within that life. Not surprisingly, there was a direct correlation between life evaluation scores and the respondent's income level relative to the people around them. By this measurement, wealth appears to provide an unlimited benefit: You can always improve your standard of living by adding more money. No one can dispute that the lifestyle of a billionaire is going to be filled with huge benefits derived directly from their income. However, the scores for people's *emotional well-being* tell a different story. Scores rose with income only until a certain level was reached ($75,000 for the group in question), after which additional income did not produce a significant additional emotional benefit.

> Increased wealth will produce an increase in *standard of living*, but once a certain threshold is reached, more money will not make us *happier*.

Research on happiness is often controversial, and results that seem to conflict with the foregoing conclusion have been presented before and will probably surface again. This is precisely because happiness, as a value, is so difficult to define and measure. Surveys that attempt it typically rely on a fixed scale to score happiness, such as 0 to 10. On that basis alone, any suggestion of a direct correlation between wealth and happiness is questionable: If a person scores their happiness as 10 out of 10, what happens when you double their income? Meanwhile, there are other indicators which challenge assumed correlations with happiness. The standard of living may be higher in richer countries, but if they also have a higher suicide rate, what does that tell you?

The concept of money was created to bridge gaps in space and time – to carry value over from the time it was earned or acquired, to the time it was spent. It has created an unparalleled ease and convenience to commercial transactions, both for the compensation of labour and the acquisition of goods and services, but the translation is not perfect. The gap that money fills between the work at one end, and the purchase of things at the other, can widen to the point where we begin to lose the connection between the effort we put in and the items we acquire. That gap has grown in other ways, as money has evolved from useful objects, to representative objects, to virtual numbers in distant computers, moving further and further away from the value systems of humans.

The value of money is not directly useful to us – instead money *represents* value that might be useful to us. Similarly, it is not really meaningful to be motivated by money – if anything, we should be motivated by what money represents. If you need a motivation, connect the money to what you will spend it on, and work from that. Otherwise, if simply having greater wealth is the objective, you'll never reach it, and you'll end up unhappy. Money is a tool, a means to an end. Having clarity over what that end is for you will give you a real motivation and an actual reward for achieving your goal.

> *We've never had it so good. We've never had so much*
> *money, we've never been so healthy, we've never lived so*
> *long as we do today. We have everything we want, and still*
> *we go around as if we were in mourning for something.*
> *– Peter Brabeck, CEO of Nestlé*

In Summary

Ask anyone in western cultures if they are in any way motivated by financial wealth, and nearly everyone would say "yes". However, dig a little deeper, and you will find that it is not the wealth, but the prospect of what that money might bring that is the true motivating force.

It is true that in our current society, the attainment of any level on Maslow's Hierarchy of Needs can be simplified by throwing money at the problem. Money can buy what we need for survival; it can also buy us property, a degree of security, and arguably even respect. In fact, money has climbed the pyramid to the point at which many people believe they need a lot more of it to have time for reflective thought and self-actualization. This thinking is a symptom of tunnel vision – an entrapment of living within a number-based value system. Beyond survival and physical security, money is not necessary to satisfy our other human needs. In a human value system, there are limitations as to what money can buy.

Herzberg's research concluded that the effect of salary on employee job attitude (and, I would infer, work-life happiness) is similarly limited, and that other factors are the true motivators. Unfortunately, the qualitative measurement of those factors makes them more difficult to quantify and/or negotiate, so all too often they take a backseat to the convenient and defensible math of employee compensation schemes.

The promise of satisfaction from wealth alone is often an empty one, since the goal, if achieved, has a frustrating habit of redefining itself and moving further away again. We believe that with a certain bank balance we will at last be happy, but when we have it, our dream balance increases and our longing continues. This is partly due to the unlimited linear math of money. You can always double it. The same cannot be said of any other human value. Nor does money map onto other values: If you have twice as much money, you can buy twice as many things, but you will not necessarily be twice as happy.

Earlier, I related how money was not a significant motivator for my personal working life. I tended to ignore salary numbers and focus on other things. That was suddenly impossible when I became self-employed, and I struggled to better define my desired relationship with money. How much did I need? How much would be enough? I felt that I had perhaps denied myself many pleasures because of the parsimonious practices of my early years. Too often, I was placing the value of *retaining my money* above the value of things that I might have acquired with it. So I arrived at this fuzzy goal, which nevertheless has proven useful to me:

"I will earn enough that money is never THE issue."

This might look like a decision to be rich, but it is quite the opposite. In fact, I intentionally interpreted this objective in two ways: (1) The pursuit of money was not to become the sole purpose of my working life – I did not want to make money for the sake of making money; and (2) I would earn enough money that I would not reject *affordable* things that I wanted *solely* because of their cost. My hope was that this goal, with both interpretations, would motivate me without dramatically altering my value system. The critical characteristic of my goal is a personal way of defining "enough".

There is strong evidence to suggest that although our standard of living will rise with wealth, our satisfaction with life will not. Yet we continue to steer our personal decisions and national policies based on such false measures of 'limitless' value. Even a higher standard of living is a short-lived illusion if our planet cannot sustain it. I suggest that it's time to re-examine our motivations and core values. Perhaps the happiest people in the world are those who are able to view money and food in the same way. You need to eat to live, but you only need so much. After that, it's time to push away from the table and focus on life's other pursuits. Alas, if only our physiology could tell us when we have made enough money!

> *People who celebrate technology say it has brought us an*
> *improved standard of living, which means greater speed,*
> *greater choice, greater leisure, and greater luxury.*
> *None of these benefits informs us about human satisfaction,*
> *happiness, security, or the ability to sustain life on earth.*
> *– Jerry Mander, American activist*

Chapter Five

The Value of Time

Labour was the first price, the original purchase-money
that was paid for all things. It was not by gold or by
silver, but by labour, that all wealth of the world was
originally purchased.
– Adam Smith, philosopher/economist (1723–90)

I GREW UP IN THE BEGINNING of the digital era. When I bought my first stereo system in 1984, I invested in one with an early model CD player instead of a record player. After all, digital sound (by numbers!) was clearer, more dynamic, and had a longer playing life. Numbers ruled!

A curious incident transpired when that CD player developed a slight skip a few years later. I took it into the repair shop, and was shocked when the technician told me to throw it out and buy a new one. The needed parts were still readily available so the age of the unit was not the issue. The problem was that it would cost me more to have him open the unit, diagnose the problem, and replace the faulty part than it would be to toss the whole player and purchase another one. It was not "worth his time" to fix it.

I thought long and hard about that incident. People getting upset about disposable diapers was not new, but the implication of disposable appliances seemed to be on a whole new level. Soon, this throwaway thinking began to show up everywhere, in everything from furniture to power tools. Increasingly, "replace" became more economical than "repair". Today, children in affluent countries grow up with the concept that most things cannot be repaired. I hear stories of teenagers throwing out shirts that have lost a button. In many cases, we adults are not much better. One need look no further than the contents of any dumpster outside a home renovation to see simple examples of this mindset. Many tons of reusable materials and hardware are hauled to the landfill every year because no business in its right mind would pay people to retrieve those scattered resources. It's simply "not worth the time".

Mind you, this is a sentiment of developed countries; the rest of the world does not always see things the same way. There is a belief in the West that today's electronics such as mobile phones cannot be repaired by a generic off-the-street technician. However, a stroll through any city in China or India will soon demonstrate that curb side mobile phone repair is precisely what happens in those societies. Repairing things is not an insurmountable technical challenge. It is a challenge of attitudes and values. Why do they still take the time to repair things in the developing world but not in wealthier countries?

In this chapter, we explore our relationship with time. We look at how the premium we put on this important resource has gone askew, and the impact this has had on both our environment and our sense of happiness.

The High Cost of Time

Among all the wonderful things that have happened to consumer products in the last 60 years, there are two less desirable trends: First, products aren't as durable as they used to be, and second, they're rarely designed to be repaired.

A key justification behind this general decline is that product quality and repair take time, and time is expensive. Indeed, the highest costs on any corporate balance sheet are typically wages and labour. When companies have a choice between *adding labour costs to save resources* versus *adding resource costs to save labour*, they usually enact the second choice. Industries in the developed world are biased towards automation and mechanization because the costs to acquire, power, and maintain such machinery are almost always less than the alternative labour costs. Thanks to modern productivity, the human time required to produce a new unit of something is often dramatically less than it would be to diagnose and correct a problem encountered by a consumer later on. The question is: Why is time so expensive relative to all the other costs?

It was not always this way. Historically, the supply of time was recognized as being unlimited, and labour was correctly perceived as a renewable resource. Consider the role that time played in constructing Europe's great cathedrals, many of which took multiple lifetimes to complete. The stunningly beautiful Milan Cathedral, with its magnificent craftsmanship and laborious detail, took more than 600 years to build. The availability of time was never considered to be a limiting factor in its creation. On a smaller scale, a walk through any antique furniture store provides evidence of pride in quality and countless hours of skill. Such pieces were built to last, and the artistry inherent in such things as hand-carved embellishments tells us that their intended value went far beyond a long-lived practicality. Back then, it seemed well worth the time to do things right and with esthetic appeal.

The values emphasized by cathedrals and solid-wood furniture – wonder, celebration, artistry, culture, pride, and quality – are all human values. Somewhere along the line, these values were pushed aside in favour of number-based values, and our economic perception of time as a resource changed. Instead of earning money for the *results* of their labour, people were increasingly paid for the *counted hours* of their labour. However, the prevalence of numbers alone does not explain why the cost of labour went up relative to the other resources needed to produce goods.

According to economic theory, if the supply of something is high and/or the demand decreases, then the price of that thing should go down. That principle is part of the *law of supply and demand*. Yet the cost of labour relative to other resources does not seem to follow this rule. The supply of labour is going up as the population increases, while the demand for labour is going down as modern efficiencies automate tasks and improve productivity. The relative cost of labour should be going down. On the flip side, the supply of practically every other natural resource on the planet is either fixed or decreasing, while our demand for materials is on the rise. The relative cost of raw materials should therefore be going up. Since an enormous proportion of our energy consumption is based on fossil fuels, the same argument can be made for energy. And yet the relationship of labour to materials and energy is such that we continue to place a higher value on conserving labour. The law of supply and demand is not predicting the reality. Why not?

I suggest this is because we continue to operate our economy under an obsolete paradigm dating back to the days when the bounties of the earth were perceived as unlimited, essentially free, and available for the taking. That is why the cost of materials and energy are relatively low. Our ever-growing economy chooses to ignore the facts: With every passing minute, society's supplies of fish, trees, fertile land, clean water, and fossil fuels go down, while its supply of labour goes up. Perhaps more importantly, when modern technology started to raise the *possible* standard of living, more people aspired to have that standard, which required an increase in individual wealth. People demanded a greater return on their labour time so that they could acquire this higher standard of living, driving the cost of labour ever higher.

Our current economic practices aim to increase productivity and reduce labour. Manufacturers, healthcare providers, schools, retailers, governments, banks, food producers – everyone is striving to do more using fewer people. This has a couple of effects: The first is that when employers use automation, efficiency, or lower quality to cut their workforces, profits become more concentrated in the hands of business owners and the few who are still working. The second effect is a level of unemployment that runs counter to our social goals. Therefore, in a hopeless attempt to keep everyone gainfully employed, we increase production and inflate the economy in other ways – resulting in our throwaway society.

> Placing a high relative value on time actually
> increases unemployment and/or demands
> unsustainable economic expansion, while
> concentrating wealth in the hands of the few.

Consider how much real wealth exists in the world, and how many things we don't do in sustainable ways because of the labour it would require. There is more than enough potential for everyone to be both happy and busy in beneficial ways. However, because our economy actively works against a practical distribution of such needs, we have to invent new ways of turning resources into short-lived goods and services just to keep the whole system pushing forward. In the financial sector, millions of people are paid handsomely just to shuffle wealth on paper. We also create new service positions and bureaucracies just to manage the machinery of the economy itself. Our economy is like a destination-less steam train riding the linear, unidirectional tracks of a number-based value system. As the train must constantly accelerate, we are either going to run out of coal or jump the tracks.

When materials are priced cheaper than time, we waste resources and create items of inferior quality. In the future, new generations will be in place to provide plenty of labour, but the materials and fossil fuels will already have gone to perpetuate our present out-of-date thinking. Hence, at some point, a shift in the value relationship between labour, materials, and energy will be unavoidable. Surely the time to start thinking about that is now. If we focused on product design, quality, reusability, and longevity instead of cheap throwaway goods, what would happen? Employment would go up, consumer satisfaction would go up, worker satisfaction would probably go up, and resource consumption would go down.

So how might this be achieved? Instead of discouraging labour (by taxing wages and charging benefit costs to employers), what if the government heavily taxed raw material extraction and stopped supplementing the cost of energy? If the planet's natural resources and energy supply were to cost more relative to labour, then reduce-reuse-recycle strategies would be more attractive and the public sector would get revenue for resources that essentially belong to the public in the first place. Instead of businesses relying on the consumption of new materials to generate profits, the emphasis would be on entirely new service sectors: repair, materials reclamation, and cradle-to-grave management (by which manufacturers are responsible for the product after it's no longer functional). Products would be designed differently if the manufacturers knew that they might be responsible for repairing and disassembling them at the end of their life. More standardized and interchangeable parts would be used. Goods might initially cost more, but they'd last longer. Who knows? We might also return to a time when pride and quality of workmanship were valued more than the ability to crank out maximum units in the minimum amount of time.

> Taxing raw material extraction instead of labour would increase market sustainability, product quality, consumer satisfaction, and employment.

This kind of thinking requires more than a shift in the way business perceives time and materials. As individuals, we also have to rethink how we value our time.

What's Your Time Worth?

The major source of wealth for most of us is through remuneration for our labour. This remuneration is a pivotal point through which individual effort, skill, experience, and talent are somehow quantified into a number – a profoundly significant translation. By setting a salary, the market instantly assigns a numeric value to some of our most personal attributes, and once this happens, our worth is quantified on the linear scale of a number-based value system. All comparisons of compensation are now absolute, and it becomes possible for the value of one person's contribution to society to be numerically compared to another's. Salaries can be correlated across any spectrum of industries; your pay scale can be directly compared to that of a professional athlete or that of your spouse, with all of the emotional effects that can entail. Any reduction in this number is often interpreted as a personal insult, regardless of fluctuations in the real value of money or of the work being performed.

The single universal scale of numbers is also perfect for inciting labour disputes, allowing workers to compare their pay scales to others in the absence of any other relevant factors. It could be an absolute difference, or it could be a relative one ("they got a 5% raise, we want one too") – whichever works to the advantage of the complainant. The numbers make it so easy that valid grievances are difficult to separate from those which might lack legitimacy.

Another potential value conflict arises when we derive income from more than one source. Our pay rates can be vastly different between different employers. Although there's sometimes an opportunity for negotiation at hiring time, the overwhelming determinant of our pay is not what our hours are worth to us, but what they are worth to our employer. And yet the term "compensation" suggests that it is the value to us that is more important. If we are to be *compensated* for our time, *what is our time actually worth?* For the answer, I turn first to my own experience.

During my first decade of full-time employment, I had been able to comfortably ignore the question of what was appropriate compensation. I worked hard (usually for far more hours than I was being paid), deposited my pay cheques, and spent less than I made, which suited me just fine. All that changed when I left the world of salaried positions and entered that of self-employment. It was not just that the income could no longer be taken for granted. The challenge was that every transaction now needed a dollar value to be negotiated and set for each situation. I struggled to set a value for my time with a number.

Self-employment had me working in a diverse mix of industries, using a host of different skills and experience. One week, I might be overseas teaching computer programming; the next I could be facilitating a management team out on a rock face. When potential clients asked me what my time was worth, I found it impossible to quote a standard number. I might earn 'x' dollars per hour working for a non-profit group, and bill ten times that amount doing essentially the same work for a corporate client. A self-employed person can either quote different wages for different situations, or turn down anything that doesn't meet a fixed number for what they decide their hours are worth. I chose the former, a flexibility that sometimes confuses people who are more directly motivated by money. They don't understand why I do work for some people at substantially lower rates than I do for others. "Surely your time is worth more than that", they say – yet another example of value system confusion.

Those who have deeply integrated money into their value system evaluate compensation in a linear way: More money is good, less money is bad. But this is not how everyone's value system operates.

Speaking for myself, my bottom line is how I feel about the amount I am being paid, relative to the amount that the other party is earning from my contribution. If I feel unfairly treated, or I feel that I am cheating someone else, I'm unhappy; otherwise, I'm satisfied. The question then becomes: "What is a fair amount to receive in this instance?" In the world of number-based value systems, determining what is *fair* is not easy.

The Elusive Idea of Fair Pay

Anyone with a sibling knows that there is no mathematical method to divide a single prized dessert into two pieces in which the fairness can't be contested. Instead, the preferred fair method is: one person cuts the dessert in two and the other person chooses their piece – the pieces don't even have to be equally sized. Perhaps the second person will choose the larger piece, perhaps not.

Fair compensation is a similarly dynamic and subjective concept. It is impossible to define fairness by formulas or ratios, but given enough other information, our innate human value systems are pretty good at telling us what seems fair and what doesn't. Unfortunately, while variable compensation might work well for the self-employed like myself, it is not a practical concept for the traditionally salaried workforce. Still, a sense of fairness must somehow be achieved if you are to truly value any compensation for your time. Your pay has a fixed value in the numeric world of dollars, but its value in human terms can vary considerably. You might be perfectly happy with your salary until you learn that a colleague doing the same work is earning substantially more. The University of Bonn brain-scanning experiments referred to in the previous chapter speak directly to this phenomenon: Any motivation or positive reaction to a monetary reward can be wiped out with the knowledge that your colleague is getting more than you.

A perception of fairness is therefore critical to the task of attracting and retaining employees. This task in itself is important, given today's mobile workforce, when many workers find it relatively easy to change jobs and even cities if they choose to. This creates a real challenge for employers: How do they determine what will be perceived as fair pay? The complexity of this challenge has inspired many schemes that can be used in workplace compensation formulas, including cost-of-living adjustments, bonuses, commissions, danger pay, predefined scales, etc. Such modifiers can help, but by far the greatest influence is exerted by the labour market itself using the *law of supply and demand*. If you can't find the employees you need, you offer more money. This *market-based compensation* is why plumbers can earn more than university graduates: There are fewer unemployed plumbers.

Letting the marketplace determine salaries might seem to be the best solution, but there's a serious flaw in that strategy – one that causes significant economic harm and leaves us with a distorted system. That flaw is our attitude towards any downward adjustment in pay. In a perfect market-driven system, governed by the law of supply and demand, compensation should fluctuate over time. If the demand for workers goes up or the supply of workers goes down, salaries should rise. Conversely, if demand goes down or supply goes up, salaries should fall. In reality, only the former effect is socially acceptable. Once a pay level is set for an employee, it is almost invariably seen as a fixed minimum; it's quite rare for existing salaries to be lowered. Even when market forces do change the prevailing rate, it is typically unacceptable to apply rates to new employees that differ from the rates paid to those already employed. If the market rates are lower, they are rejected; if they are higher, everyone must move up at the same time.

Of course, such biases do not apply to the company's prospects: Its business revenue is subject to the standard supply and demand factors of the marketplace. Yet, the same selective application of market effects is seen with the division of that revenue: When a company's profitability increases, workers usually insist on a raise; but when the company is less profitable, a pay cut will still be vigorously contested. Sadly, one impact of this is that downturns are often experienced as all or nothing: either no salary change or a loss of job.

This aversion to salary reductions is one of the main reasons why economists believe moderate inflation to be a desirable attribute of any economy. Since the labour force will aggressively oppose any literal reduction in their income, managers of the economy use inflation to achieve the same effect by making those payroll dollars worth less.

Thus the market can rebalance using math that isn't as obvious to the average worker.

Remuneration for the 1%

Market-based compensation has another flaw: It only works where fair market forces can be applied. This is clearly not the case in the top enclaves of society. Society's richest came to be known as "the 1%" back when 1% of the population was making 10% of the world's total income. Now they are making 20%, while 8% of the world's wealth is held by just the top 0.1%. How does this happen? Economic theory is sometimes used to justify huge compensation packages, but when we look more closely, the valuation of time simply doesn't add up.

"Very high salaries are the only way to attract the very best."

When suitable candidates are in short supply, lucrative compensation packages are indeed one way to attract the top talent. For professional athletes at the top of their game, high salaries are tied to demonstrated excellence in a sport, but only if that sport generates sufficient revenues to support such payrolls. (Women's hockey leagues, for example, presumably attract the very best by some other means.) Remuneration for star athletes is determined by what they can demand, and high ticket prices soon follow. Given the direct connection between the revenues of the team owners, the salaries of the players, and the attendance of the fans, professional sports do operate in a viable market-based fashion. We increasingly see evidence of this as lock-outs and strikes occur in professional sports and salaries start to be capped. The system is somewhat self-regulating, but only within the very limited sports market. Salaries say nothing about the societal value of a professional basketball player compared to that of a cardiac surgeon, for example.

A similar phenomenon can be observed with corporate CEOs, except that market forces do not apply as they did for the athletes. While compensation for CEOs and the like are technically determined by the shareholders, the disconnect between shareholders and the board of directors in large corporations typically renders this determination meaningless. That means that with only the support of the board, CEO compensation can rapidly soar upward unchecked.

How can the market ever adjust their salaries downward? The law of supply and demand only works when the market has sufficient options to vote with its wallet. If full access to top level positions is not an open market, and salary determination is too far removed from shareholders or market influence (or even actual revenues), then the high salaries are not being used to attract the best players in a free market – they are simply a cash grab by a privileged group.

"These CEOs are actually worth the money they make."

Here's a typical scenario: A multi-billion dollar company is losing $300 million dollars a year. A new CEO is brought on board – a talented and tough individual who cuts the workforce by a third and makes other difficult decisions. The next year, the company turns around and starts making a $500 million profit. It will be argued that this one individual created $800 million of value for the company, so paying them $40 million a year is a mere 5% of the value they created.

However, this is just a mathematical shell game, making inappropriate use of percentages. Firstly, to justify compensation in such proportional terms, it should be based on those terms. If the company had lost $800 million in the CEO's first year at the helm, would the CEO have paid 5% of that back out of their own pocket? Not a chance. (Indeed, phenomenal salaries for executives leading companies that are losing money are particularly irksome to shareholders.) Top executives won't be held monetarily responsible for a loss, but they will take all the credit for a gain.

Secondly, within a typical company, none of the other salaries are justified by the value of the overall corporate balance sheet. Granted, leading a larger company calls for better skills than leading a smaller operation, but it is a stretch to think that a company fifty times as big as another company would demand fifty times the effort or talent in the top job – yet, the value-percentage argument suggests that the CEO should receive fifty times the compensation.

Furthermore, it is disturbing when corporate executives are handsomely rewarded for improving a company's bottom line at the cost of job losses, plant closures, and actions that show little social or environmental responsibility. Which values are being rewarded and encouraged here?

> *The salary of the chief executive of a large corporation is*
> *not a market award for achievement. It is frequently in the*
> *nature of a warm personal gesture by the individual to*
> *himself.* – *John Kenneth Galbraith, economist (1908-2006)*

Keep in mind that whether we are talking about upper management, athletes, plumbers, or cardiac surgeons, the fairness of anyone's compensation is something that is decided between the employee(s) and the employer; whether or not the rest of society believes it to be fair is immaterial. Our numeric salary is based on our value to the employer in that specific relationship – it says nothing about our value to society.

Furthermore, since our working hours are typically priced at their value to those paying us, what we earn in that relationship says nothing about the value of our time to ourselves. If asked to describe the value we attribute to our non-working hours, we would not do so in terms of dollars and cents. It is important then to recognize that commercial and personal ways of valuing time are not the same. When we adopt a number-based value for time, we often begin to apply inappropriate commercial objectives like 'saving time' to our own lives, resulting in even more value collisions.

Saving Time

"Remember that time is money", wrote Benjamin Franklin over 250 years ago in his <u>Advice to a Young Tradesman</u>. What he was referring to is the *opportunity cost* of time: If you can earn $40 in an hour, and you take two hours off, that will 'cost' you $80. Unproductive labour, inefficiencies, delays, idle machinery – all of these can represent an opportunity cost to a business venture. In the number-based world of commerce, time is an extremely important resource, and it is possible to objectively assign a dollar value to every hour. This has led to the wide-spread perception of time as an opportunity to be monetarily productive or else wasted. Unfortunately this thinking has crept into our personal valuations of time, distorting how we spend our 'off-hours' in some disturbing ways.

Since the business world treats time as a cost, modern marketing is constantly promoting the idea that any task in life can be improved by conveniences that reduce the task-time required. No doubt our standard of living by most measures is generally higher than at any time in our history. However, this obsession with saving time puts other values at risk. Take the simple example of food: In the United States of 1870, it is estimated that 70-80% of the population was employed in agriculture. That figure is now down to 2-3%. We now have industrial agriculture and people in other countries specializing in growing, transporting, and storing our food so that we don't have to. This phenomenal change in the effort required to put food into ourselves is observable at more than just the production stage. Too often, we no longer know where our food comes from, what's in it, or the joy that comes from preparing it. Chef Jamie Oliver claims that some American families are now into their second (or even third) generation of people who don't have the basic kitchen skills required to turn raw ingredients into a healthy meal. The impacts of prepared and processed foods are profound. Not only are we not taking the time to prepare and enjoy our food, but there is also a decline in the social practice of families sitting down to a meal together at the same time. All of this is driven in part by the pressure to save time, do more with less, and maximize our hours at work.

If food is seen as a tiresome but necessary refuelling in order to get back to life, what are we doing with that life? Is it not ironic that at one point Farmville, the hit online agricultural simulation game, had over 110 million players? Active users were collectively spending more than 20 million hours and over $1 million of real money *every day* to grow virtual crops that fed no one (except indirectly the game's creators).

> *Modern man thinks he loses something – time – when he*
> *does not do things quickly. Yet he does not know what to do*
> *with the time he gains – except kill it.*
> *– Erich Fromm, sociologist (1900–80)*

Modern efficiencies mean that we are theoretically able to devote less time per person to meet basic survival needs. That means that, as a society, we have a lot of surplus time not required for our survival. And yet anthropologists claim that we actually work much longer hours now than our hunter-gatherer ancestors of a few thousand years ago. It's estimated that skilled foragers could collect one week's worth of food in about 3 hours! The structure of our modern economy is such that we have made it impossible for most people to thrive without enormous effort. Instead of using that surplus time to better ourselves and the world around us, we struggle to find ways to keep ourselves busy in order to pay ourselves. How can it be that we have more time-saving devices than any generation before us, and yet our forefathers seem to have had so much more time to enjoy life? Is our longer lifespan truly worth the effort it takes to fund it? It's odd to say that we now enjoy 20 more years of life compared to the pre-Industrial Age if we can no longer enjoy the first 60. This calls to mind the *Parable of the Mexican Fisherman*, who was criticized for taking too many days off and spending too much of his time relaxing and enjoying his family life. The argument went that if he worked harder, caught more fish, built up his fleet, and hired more people, then decades later he could eventually retire, work fewer days, and spend more time relaxing with his family!

Time is a resource whose limit matters to us intimately. We know that our individual supply of time is finite, but we don't know exactly how much we have. All we know is that every second, we have less than we did before. If we make the error of applying economic principles to such a strictly limited personal resource, its monetary value should be high. Furthermore, maximum benefit should be achieved by saving hours wherever possible and by maximizing their derived benefit. While that might make sense from a business perspective, when we apply those principles to our personal lives, we attempt to do everything faster and earn the most dollars for our labour – even if that makes us stressed, dissatisfied, and unhealthy. Alas, we are applying number-based value principles to a personal resource that should be valued *qualitatively*, not *quantitatively*. Even though our individually limited *quantity* of time suggests that each and every hour should be of high value, in fact we only truly desire the hours when we are extracting pleasure from our time. An hour of happiness is more desirable to a person (hence more valuable) than an hour of misery. This is a qualitative distinction which calls for completely different principles to maximize our ultimate satisfaction from life.

> *There is more to life than increasing its speed.*
> – *Mahatma Gandhi, Indian nationalist leader (1869–1948)*

Getting the Balance Right

Let's assume that a useful goal is to maximize the benefit of the limited hours that make up our lifetime. While most of us would place a higher personal value on the hours when we are not working, we also know that work hours allow us to pay for necessities and buy things that help us to better enjoy our lives. Still, we need to realize that such investments are subject to the *law of diminishing returns*.

For example, in the commercial world where financial return is the ultimate goal, businesses can sometimes increase that return by investing employee work-hours in 'unproductive' things like training or goodwill gestures. While such actions have a short-term opportunity cost, they can have a long-term benefit. However, this benefit has a limit, after which the additional return diminishes and will not justify the time invested. The idea is to find the work/training balance that gives the peak benefit. The same law of diminishing returns applies to a personal world in which maximum happiness is the ultimate goal. We can increase the payoff of that goal by investing parts of our life in 'less happy' pursuits such as working for others, but if we invest too many work-hours in the pursuit of wealth, our happiness-return will diminish. There is a point at which the satisfaction-value of additional income will be offset by the hours spent earning it.

> The investment of money-earning hours to increase your happiness has a peak value, after which additional hours produce the opposite effect.

Many in lower income brackets have not yet reached that peak satisfaction point, but others are well past it. Recognizing that such a point exists is the first step for those seeking a better work/life balance. An even more powerful realization for most of us in the developed world is that this balance point, which indicates our *maximum quality of life*, can be adjusted up or down, partly based on how much we tie our happiness to wealth. The standard of living we choose for ourselves can determine how much income we need in order to maintain it, so we can minimize the work hours required. Unfortunately, we tend to do the opposite:

We maximize our work hours and then let our income determine our standard of living.

Even if we actively choose a realistic standard of living, we may still put too much stress on maximizing our hourly wage in order to minimize the hours invested. Since we can always potentially earn more money per hour, how do we know when a satisfactory level has been reached? When do we stop changing jobs or going on strike or scrambling for a promotion to the next pay level? The problem is that there is no such thing as a maximum possible income. In the absence of any inherent concept of 'sufficiency' in numbers, we're better off to use some other non-numeric value to determine when enough is enough.

Imagine a society in which everyone was paid for labour at the same hourly rate. No, I am not proposing this as a Utopian solution, just as a mental exercise. Give it a try. If you were just graduating from high school, think about how you would select your career path. If you were a worker in this environment, how would your vocational aspirations change? If you were managing a business in this society, how would you attract the talent and skills you needed? In all these scenarios, other values become more pronounced. What would they be for you? Perhaps as a graduate, you would think about what excited you instead of what produced the highest income. As a worker, you might forego a promotion and switch departments instead. As an employer, you might make your workplace less stressful to attract deep thinkers. A world in which all salaries are identical is not going to happen any time soon, but that does not prevent us from identifying the alternate values uncovered by such thinking – and reaping the benefits that come with putting more emphasis on them.

Valuing Time on Your Own Terms

Like many people of his generation, my father retired around the age of 65. He had worked steadily as a human geneticist, seeing patients, managing a cytogenetics laboratory, and being an active member of various university committees. After his retirement, he gave up his office in town, and a large number of boxes of papers and files came home. That was the only change that anyone noticed. He continued to work the same long hours, ostensibly doing all of the same things that he used to do, day in and day out. His example was not entirely unique; I started to meet other similarly 'retired' people who continued to work as if nothing had changed. I asked them what it meant to be retired, since I could not see the difference in their lives.

The consensus seemed to be that they no longer *had* to go into the office every day, but they *chose* to do so. Most had reached a level of financial self-sufficiency and could stop working if they wanted to, but they didn't want to give up everything completely. However, they did take advantage of their newfound freedom. If a travel opportunity or an interesting project presented itself, they could drop everything else and take it up. Retirement did not mean the end of working; it meant valuing time on their own terms.

This way of life intrigued me. Although I did not have their retirement packages and pension plans, I was a debt-free homeowner, due to the lifestyle described in the previous chapter. I couldn't see why I had to wait until I was 65 to adopt their approach. So, shortly before my fortieth birthday, I announced that I was "retired". I was already a self-employed consultant, and, like my father, I did not stop working for clients or billing for my time. After all, I still had the usual bills to pay and I was in no position to live off my savings for the rest of my life. I still worked, but I revisited what work I was willing to do and under what conditions. Perhaps it would be better to call it a *re-evaluation* than a retirement. I told my clients that when I was on-site in their offices, they would have my complete attention, but when I was home, my time might not be for sale. I avoided inflexible full-time or long-term contracts, and did not take on projects that held no interest for me. As might be expected, my income and *standard of living* went down. But more to the point, my *quality of life* went up. I don't deny that my situation is unique: The socio-economic realities of today's world mean that such choices are just not available to many people. However, I do believe that the insights gained are generally applicable to most of us.

> *It is good to have money and the things that money can buy,*
> *but it's good too, to check up once in a while and make sure*
> *you haven't lost the things money can't buy.*
> *– George Lorimer, editor (1867–1937)*

My opening premise for this chapter was that society's supply of time is virtually unlimited and hence overvalued relative to other resources such as materials and energy. Contrast this with each individual's limited allotment of life hours, each to be treasured. How might it be possible for individuals and society to have compatible perspectives on the value of time if the resource is at once finite, and thus highly valued, and also boundless, and therefore of lower value? How could it be possible for society to value time as I suggest it should? It turns out that this is quite simple to resolve. We each need to value our time differently from the way in which society or businesses value our time.

Our society typically values an individual's time in *quantitative* terms – the number of labour-hours spent performing productive tasks. Therefore, society's benefit can be maximized by increasing the hours that are spent by all of us for the good of society, including both paid and unpaid work time. In contrast, as individuals, we innately value our time in *qualitative* terms, so our benefit can be maximized by increasing the satisfaction with which each hour is spent. Since humans have a built-in tendency to regard socially collaborative behaviours as a satisfying use of our time, these two valuation systems actually support one another. In other words, the time we spend for the good of society is rewarding to both ourselves and society – even if in some cases we're not paid for it. When that happens, civilization gets the time-input that it needs to maintain a good standard of living for all, and individuals get the satisfaction that comes from working together, contributing to a greater good, and feeling valued.

I fully appreciate the benefits of wealth and full employment, but individuals rarely starve in self-sufficient communities where everyone knows and looks out for one another. If, on the other hand, we continue to adopt an increasingly quantitative valuation of time, putting in overtime, squandering barrels of oil and even more time in commuting, and working jobs that are getting tougher to hold on to, then we get incompatibilities which contribute to our current value crisis. The more we step away from evaluating our time and labour by monetary compensation alone, the more we can contribute to society and our own quality of life in meaningful ways.

In Summary

Time is a unique resource, its supply being both limited for individuals and almost unlimited for society. Yet our economy treats time as if it were a preciously limited commodity: Because it is highly priced, every effort is made to 'save' it. In the meantime, we as individuals have taken to applying economic valuations of time in our personal lives. We feel intense pressure to save time, increase productivity, and maximize our wealth, often at the sacrifice of being happy. Somewhere along the line, our value system wires have gotten crossed.

For the majority of us, time is our most significant individual commodity to be sold, and therefore our most significant entrance into the number-based value system of money. Income is obviously important as the medium that translates our labour into food and shelter, but once basic needs are met, the significance of the remainder takes on a different dimension. The level of compensation for our time can be falsely perceived as our personal value to society – what we are worth, compared to our neighbour. When our remuneration is simply a number, such comparisons become unavoidable, as are the perceptions of imbalance or unfairness that actually diminish the value of our pay in human terms. As a consequence, we allow our bank balance to determine our self-worth, and dismiss other values in the pursuit of increasing the monetary return on the hours of our lives.

Meanwhile, the high cost of labour relative to the cost of natural resources and energy has resulted in a disposable society. In order to keep the economy growing, businesses manufacture cheap, low-quality goods that don't last or are thrown away while still 98% functional because it costs too much to repair them. Raw materials and energy are voraciously consumed to support that effort. Yet this trend is rewarded within a monetary value system, as planned obsolescence and repeat sales of the same product lead to increased profits. There are many better, healthier, and more sustainable ways of doing things – choices that will never be made under the current paradigm because they 'cost too much' or would be 'a waste of time'. The way we value time over our own environment makes no sense.

Within an economic framework, the value of time is quantified as salaries and opportunity costs. In the absence of such a framework, the value of time is determined by how we spend it. I like the idea that "time is money", but not in the way in which Benjamin Franklin intended it. I think we should treat time the same way that we should treat money – not valuing it for itself, but valuing what we can get from spending it wisely. There is no more value to obsessively saving time than there is to obsessively saving money. In both cases, you can't take it with you when you go.

I consider myself very fortunate to have stumbled upon my unusual 'retirement' concept (popularly known as *voluntary simplicity*), and to live in circumstances in which I could make it happen. I now consider the value of time more frequently in terms of my own personal values – how much I treasure my hours and what I do with them. Declaring a state of pseudo-retirement has brought about a drop in my standard of living, but the benefits have been worth it. For one thing, I'd never have otherwise been able to take on the challenge of writing this book.

Ironically, in the middle of writing my final version, the power supply in one of my flat screen monitors failed. While all of the fantastically complicated little pixels that make up my multi-coloured computer reality were still functioning, one small power component was burnt out somewhere. Asking where I might have it repaired would probably have subjected me to ridicule and incredulity. The economy wanted me to throw this monitor out and buy a new one. Fortunately, a simple internet repair video had a different idea. Perhaps my next retirement project will be spending some time learning to repair more electronics. I would like that.

> *Time is the coin of your life. It is the only coin you have, and*
> *only you can determine how it will be spent. Be careful lest*
> *you let other people spend it for you.*
> *– Carl Sandburg, American poet (1878–1967)*

Chapter Six

Banking on Numbers

All money is a matter of belief.
– Adam Smith, philosopher/economist (1723–90)

MY EARLIEST ENCOUNTER WITH the stock market was a one-time investment orchestrated by my father when I was in my teens. He bought five thousand shares in a resource company and then transferred them to me, possibly as an experiment in saving taxes on capital gains. Within a couple of months, the share value increased from $1.20 to $1.70, at which point the shares were sold. I have no recollection of what happened to that 'found money', but one thing was crystal clear: We had just made $2,500 in two months, having done absolutely nothing to earn it.

My next stock market transaction, many years later, was a total embarrassment. I had put an ad in the paper for a General Manager to take the growing independent software company I worked for to the next level. Unbeknownst to me, unscrupulous stock brokers trolled the classified ads for just such contact information, and I was suddenly on the receiving end of an extremely high-pressure sales pitch to invest in some stocks. Like many victims of scams, in hindsight I can't quite fathom why I allowed it happen, but I made two separate purchases of shares in the energy sector and held them for some time before their value wavered and eventually dropped to insignificance. Since then, I have limited my investing to mutual funds, mostly within the registered retirement savings plans (RRSPs) common in Canada. I don't follow the markets, I don't move stuff around much, and so it may come as no surprise (especially in the volatile markets of the last 20 years) that my returns have been below par, if not below zero.

My poor investment returns are perhaps poetic justice for a lifetime of non-participation in the economy. I have to face this simple fact: The economy hates me and my value system. Why? Because I stifle economic growth. Instead of consuming, I save. I obsessively reduce, reuse, and recycle everything possible. I have never had a student loan, a car loan, or a business loan. I have never carried a credit card balance. My mortgage was paid off in 1999, and in economic terms, my inputs and outputs are ridiculously small. I received my last employee pay cheque in March 1992 and my annual income has been in steady decline ever since, without even accounting for inflation. And yet I live a comfortable existence with few concerns for the future, not because of how much I have, but because of how little I need.

It wasn't until I started this book that I realized how 'unnatural' my behaviour is in a contemporary economy. This inspired me to wonder: Just how *natural* is our concept of an economy? In this chapter, we will explore the disconnect between real and monetary values, and learn how this has led to disastrous financial meltdowns. Though we commonly believe that we can navigate the ebbs and flows of our modern day economy, this chapter will show that unless we make some deep changes soon, the worst is inevitably and irrevocably yet to come.

Economic Nature

The term "economy" is derived from the Greek word *oikonomia*, which simply means *household management*. One can imagine that the word developed quite naturally in the human lexicon as families organized themselves within communities, balancing the inputs and outputs needed for a harmonious survival. Indeed, some of our modern economic theories appear to be grounded in the natural behaviour of humans and other species. Behaviours consistent with the *law of supply and demand*, for example, are common in the animal kingdom. When the supply of something like a particular food source goes down, its value – the lengths to which animals will go to get it – goes up. Similarly, when populations rise and fall, varying the demand for space, defended territories shrink and expand accordingly.

Foraging animals exhibit clear demonstrations of the *marginal value theory*, consuming just the low-hanging fruit and then moving on, so long as there are other trees to harvest. Other economic concepts are echoed in insect species, which have many examples of industrious colonies with class hierarchies, specialized labour, and even primitive implementations of agriculture. Studies of primates have established innate ideals of reciprocity and collaboration, in which family units and bands will work together for the common good. These advancements all appear to be a natural consequence of evolving sophistication.

However, it would be a stretch to suggest that any other species has an 'economy'. While their behaviours can be modeled by mathematical formulas, no other species relies on numbers, nor are they driven by math. In contrast, human society is now profoundly entrenched in a number-based value system. The economy concept, and especially our concerted effort to manage it, is an invention of mankind.

For centuries, society refined its mantra on the economy until it reached the stage we are at now – a ubiquitous acceptance across the planet that economic growth is somehow necessary for our existence. Everything is focused on growing the economy: government policies, commercial activities, hours of labour, investment markets, fashion, technology, and consumer mindsets. Why is this so? Firstly, because there is a clear correlation between economic growth and our standard of living. If we choose to maintain our current standard of living, economic growth has to at least match the growth of the population. A more ominous and less well-known reason is that economic growth is necessary to create wealth to pay the interest on loans – a potentially ruinous challenge that will be explored later in this chapter.

Since there is no question that humanity has benefited from economic growth in the past, it's very difficult to question the paradigm of economic growth for our future. However, continued growth from limited resources is simply impossible. The thin skin of resources on this planet cannot sustain the old way of doing things for much longer. Unfortunately, it may take a few more crises like the financial ones experienced in recent years to drive that message home.

In previous chapters we discussed the unique properties of numbers – namely that they are linear, consistent, and limitless – and how those properties are inherited by number-based value systems, such as money. They give money the ability to be calculable, to cross borders, and to represent any quantity imaginable (and unimaginable!), making it an extremely useful and powerful tool. That power has allowed civilization to do remarkable things, but the properties that are money's strengths are also its weaknesses. Linearity is restrictive, consistency is inflexible, and limitlessness applies to the good and the bad. Let's look at some specific historical examples of what can happen when economic numbers spin completely out of control.

The Balloon Economy

When the idea of money was first introduced, it took the form of small items of tangible value that everyone in a given population recognized as useful. To tamper with such value would be very difficult. If I am paying you with a goat or a bag of rice, you can see for yourself the value of what you are getting. But when money later moved to objects that represented wealth, the whole system had to rely on a new layer of trust – the belief that the object would retain its initial value and could be used by the recipient to acquire something of equal real value. A representative currency is convenient, but it is also risky. If the participants in an economy no longer trust the value that their money represents, that value will drop. Any drop in the real value of a currency is called *inflation*, because prices for real goods and services will 'inflate' to compensate for the reduced currency value. Simply put, your dollar cannot buy what it did before.

Most of society is now quite familiar with the term "inflation". Economists consider low, positive, non-zero inflation to be necessary for the management of a healthy economy. However, inflation itself is not always manageable. Being driven by numbers with no inherent limits, economies can sometimes explode into *hyperinflation*: inflation that's out of control. Hyperinflation usually happens when a country's central monetary authority, responsible for the printing of its currency, is forced to increase the money supply to levels inconsistent with the value of the economy. In other words, the 'paper wealth' of the country goes up dramatically, while the real wealth remains the same. The idea is pretty much equivalent to a person who writes a cheque for money that they don't have – sooner or later, the market is going to notice.

Flipping through history, I found over fifty examples of hyper-inflation spread across the globe. All but two of these economic crises have happened since 1914, and more than two-thirds occurred in just the past thirty years. Let me begin with the most extreme example that I could uncover: the economic collapse of Hungary in 1946. Hungary had already suffered a separate bout of hyperinflation in the early 1920s as a consequence of the First World War. The government resorted to printing excess money to pay its debts, which resulted in a monthly inflation rate of 98 percent. That means that in 1922, prices doubled every month. Even that pales in comparison to what happened in response to a similar state of debt after the Second World War. In 1945, Hungary's national currency, the pengő, lost so much value that even the highest denomination note – the 1,000 pengő bill – could not buy a loaf of bread. To allow commerce to continue, the government began printing bills in increasingly larger denominations, leading to a 10,000,000 pengő bill by the end of 1945. At its peak, the inflation rate was the highest ever recorded: 13 quadrillion percent per month, meaning that prices doubled every 15 hours.

Even as the pengő and all of Hungary's printed money reached completely absurd levels of worthlessness, the limitless number scale was able to keep pace as if there was nothing wrong – the system simply added zeroes. Just months after the 10-million pengő bill was introduced, the Hungarian government was printing the highest denomination of this (or any other) currency: the 100-quintillion (100,000,000,000,000,000,000) pengő bill. By the time the pengő was finally abandoned, mathematicians had allegedly calculated the total value of all Hungarian printed currency combined to be about one-tenth of a U.S. cent. One might argue that the paper the money was printed on was worth more than that.

Hyperinflation is not just a feature of history. Second only to Hungary's record was Zimbabwe's more recent 79.6 billion percent monthly inflation rate, with prices doubling every day. Today's news tends to quote *annualized* inflation rates, which for Zimbabwe as of December 2008 would have been 6.5 quindecillion novemdecillion percent. (That number is 650 million googol or 65 followed by 107 zeroes. You can derive a similar number by multiplying the estimated number of atoms in the universe by the estimated diameter of the observable universe in metres.) To annualize Hungary's worst monthly rate, we'd have to triple the 650 million googol and then add 62 more zeroes. Do you see how inconceivably ridiculous this all gets?

The explanation for this outrageous monetary behaviour is that the mathematics it is based on is not in any way constrained by the bounds of common sense. Once you create systems that adhere to numeric principles, you are at the mercy of their laws. Episodes of hyperinflation cause misery and hardship for entire nations; they can drive whole populations into poverty without changing their assets or their aptitude for work. Hyperinflation is not a natural disaster or one inflicted by others (although some claim that it can be orchestrated as a weapon). It is entirely a crisis of valuation, in which real values become completely disconnected from monetary ones, simply because of our reliance on the limitlessness of numbers. There's a pattern to the instigation of our past hyperinflation spirals: a national crisis (typically a war), followed by an attempt to pay for its costs or consequences, in an economy based on paper currency. It is a sobering thought that it might be even easier for hyperinflation to occur in a paperless system.

Since hyperinflation requires the creation of money for which no corresponding value exists, it is tempting to think that we could easily avoid such a crisis by abolishing the practice of creating money with no value to back it up. Unfortunately, the practice in question is precisely what our banking system has been based on for hundreds of years.

Money as Debt

Earlier in this book, I offered a brief history of money. When it was first introduced, money was used as a storage of *past value*. In other words, the item or service of value existed first, and the money recorded the transfer of that value for later use. In order to get money, one first had to carry out labour or present an item to be sold. Later, when money became an object that merely represented wealth, the opportunity arose to *create* wealth by creating the representative object – with nothing of value to back it up. This is akin to writing bad cheques, but doing so legally and without penalty. You might be surprised to learn that this is now the basis of our entire monetary system. Almost all money in existence today is a storage of *future anticipated value*. We have moved from the concept of "money as existing value" to "money as debt".

Have you ever considered how so many people, companies, and entire countries can all be in debt? Where did this borrowed money come from? Indeed, ask people where money in general comes from and you may get a number of different answers: the government, labour, natural resources, etc. These are all correct to a certain extent, but they fall short of the mark. The real answer is that most money is created by our banks, and it only exists as debt. Less than 1% of all the money now in circulation exists as printed notes or coins. More than 99% exists as nothing more than a promise to pay back money that never existed in the first place.

> More than 99% of the money in our economy is created by banks through loans, representing future value that *does not yet exist*.

For the past 300 years or so, banks have employed a mathematical sleight-of-hand called the *fractional reserve system*, which allows them to lend more money than they have on deposit. The fractional reserve system is an arbitrary invention, used to increase the money supply and facilitate economic growth – and bank profit. Under this system, banks need only keep a percentage *reserve* (traditionally 10%) of all deposits they receive, and are free to lend out the rest (the other 90%). If we apply this concept to the bank's own initial capital, they can start with $1000 of their own real money, deposit it as the retained 10% with a central bank, and then loan up to $9000 of *newly created* 'money' as *credit* to a borrower. Since they still have their original $1000 balance, this new money comes not from deposits or earnings, but is created directly from the borrower's promise to repay the loan. Since money loaned is typically re-deposited in another part of the system, that $9000 deposit would allow another bank to lend up to $8100 (90%). This process feeds itself, so that every dollar deposited can result in almost ten dollars being added to the money supply, and the original $1000 in actual banker's cash can produce just under $90,000 in new debt. There is nothing held in reserve to justify the value of that new debt beyond a belief that borrowers will continue to put in the labour and raw resources to pay back into the never-ending cycle of debt.

> *I am afraid that the ordinary citizen will not like to be told*
> *that banks can and do create money. And they who control*
> *the credit of the nation direct the policy of the governments*
> *and hold in the hollow of their hands the destiny of the*
> *people. - Reginald McKenna, past chairman of the board,*
> *Midlands Bank of England*

While the required *reserve* ratio puts a limit on how much new money can be created in this fashion, the percentage varies worldwide, mostly at less than 10%. This free rein to create money is a phenomenal power which our governments have assigned to our banking system. When you want to borrow money (and that must happen for the whole system to work), the banks can create virtually unlimited wealth – with the stroke of your pen. The created wealth must then be turned into real wealth via labour or resources by *you*, not them. This in itself does not make the banks rich; as the loan is paid back, the 'created money' disappears. The catch is that only the principal disappears; any interest on the loan is retained by the bank as profit. So where does the money come from to pay the interest on all this debt? It can only come from growth in the real economy, which means from perpetual consumption of the world's supply of energy and resources. More and more raw materials have to be processed, sold, discarded, and replaced, without end, just to keep the system from collapsing.

Since the repayment of loans removes that money from existence again, and the borrowers have to create real value to cover the interest, we don't automatically get hyperinflation from this practice of creating money from nothing. However, because the money supply must constantly grow, overall gradual inflation is a near certainty. Unless your savings are growing with interest at the kind of rate that the banks are earning, those savings are continually, with every passing day, worth less than the day before.

The money in this system represents future value. If that future value cannot be created fast enough to feed back into the system, we risk a total financial meltdown. This is a major contributing factor to our present global financial crisis, and it is only going to get worse. That's because the formulas associated with these monetary policies are all *exponential functions* – a concept whose full implications the human race is notoriously bad at grasping. One thing is for certain: Our global system of creating debt money from nothing and requiring the planet to cough up the balance in raw resources is entirely unsustainable.

General ignorance of how this system works is the only thing holding it together. Were the majority of the population fully aware of how untenable it all is, the collapse could be devastating. Money has value only if we believe it has value. We have learned what happens when confidence in that belief system is shaken. The Great Depression of the 1930s was largely the result of a loss of faith in the monetary system, partly due to a dip in our agricultural output. People stopped borrowing, which resulted in a 27% reduction of the money supply from 1929 to 1933. (Note the direct relationship between borrowing and supply.) People no longer trusted that the money would be there for them; they wanted to see it and have it, causing the banks to fail. Investment stopped, and the economy – as well as people's lives – collapsed. It may have been the first near-global disaster entirely of our own creation that did not involve war. Indeed, war is what pulled the affected nations out of the crisis.

There is another interesting factor of the Great Depression which brought ruin and poverty to many. As the economy attempted to adjust to the crisis, prices and wages fell, but debt balances did not. In other words, your wage may have dropped by 60% (the average drop between 1929 and 1933), and the price of your groceries would also have gone down, but your mortgage balance and payments remained the same. Economic principles could alter prices and wages, but the relative cost of debts soared because there was no mechanism in place to adjust existing balances. A loan payment that once constituted a week's wages was now more than two weeks' wages. This phenomenon alone wiped out thousands of livelihoods. In the face of economic and social factors, the inflexible math could not match reality.

> *Debts are subject to the laws of mathematics rather than*
> *physics. Unlike wealth, which is subject to the laws of*
> *thermodynamics, debts do not rot with old age and are not*

> *consumed in the process of living. On the contrary, they*
> *grow at so much per cent per annum, by the well-known*
> *mathematical laws of simple and compound interest. [...]*
> *It is this underlying confusion between wealth and debt*
> *which has made such a tragedy of the scientific era.*
> *– Frederick Soddy, Nobel laureate (1877–1956)*

Betting the Bank

In more recent times, we have seen a series of financial crises that have unveiled appalling abuses of debt shuffling and mismanagement – a house of cards that was primed for an inevitable collapse. In a world where money represents future value, an economy driven by loans and debt is critically dependent on that value being found and taken into the system to balance the books. Lenders should therefore only make loans when there is sufficient assurance that they will be repaid by the borrowers. But in the last decade, a new business model emerged that added another layer to the value chain. Instead of waiting for the borrowers to come up with the money that the banks had created with loan agreements, the banks started selling the actual agreements to other financial institutions. The immediate effect was that the lenders cared less who they loaned to because they made their money back by selling the loan contracts, not by being repaid by the borrowers. The reliability of the borrowers, the value of any collateral, and the likelihood of repayment all diminished in importance. Inevitably, the buyers of these *debt instruments* were the mutual and pension funds that represented the financial security of the general population.

Mortgage derivatives played a key role in the financial crisis of 2008, the effects of which continue to be felt. A *derivative* is a contract between two parties that specifies dates and payments based on the values of certain specified variables. If this sounds all-encompassing and non-specific, that's because it is. They were originally called derivatives because their value was derived from the value of the under-lying assets involved. An *interest rate cap derivative*, for example, might be an agreement between two people or organizations in which one will receive a payment from the other for each month in which a specified variable interest rate exceeds 3%. A borrower who is paying a variable rate on a loan can protect herself against a rise in rates by purchasing an interest rate cap derivative. If the interest rate exceeds 3% in a given period, the payment from the derivative can be used to help make the interest payment for that period. Thus the interest payments are effectively 'capped' at 3% from the borrower's point of view. The seller of the derivative need not be connected to the original loan in any way. The relationship is conceptually similar to a gambler and a bookmaker; the derivative is a bet placed on a *subject variable* (in this case, an interest rate). In practice, the *subject variables* can be anything, ranging from the price of wheat to the weather. Furthermore, once this bet is agreed to and exists, the bet itself is considered a sellable asset – an obligation that can be bought and sold.

If you find the whole concept a bit hard to follow, don't worry – the complexity of these instruments can be mind-boggling. For example, one common practice is for investors to use derivatives to bet against their own investments. By purchasing a derivative with the value of their investment as the subject variable, they can offset (or *hedge*) their losses (if that value goes down) with the payoff from the derivative, making it act like an insurance policy. Most importantly, an investor (and, simultaneously, any number of other investors) can create a derivative for an asset that they don't even own, so long as someone is willing to take the bet. This is comparable to everyone in your neighbourhood being allowed to take out a fire insurance policy against your home. Can you guess where that might lead?

Derivative trading is nothing short of unregulated gambling, conducted on a massive scale in stock exchanges and privately throughout the world. The most dangerous aspect of this kind of gambling is that those doing it are very often betting other people's money. Furthermore, derivatives can be based on derivatives, so the cumulative risks may themselves be compounded to the point that an unusual but relatively innocuous event can have a cascading impact. Such risks, which exceed those of normal investing, are borne but rarely endorsed by those whose entire life's savings might be on the line. We now have instances of rogue traders single-handedly losing multiple billions of dollars and bringing entire financial institutions to ruin – one person decimating the life savings and livelihoods of thousands. Such gambles are played out as just a numbers game. True values are difficult to discern until the final effect arrives at the doorstep of the individual contributors, who lose so much. And yet the popularity of derivative trading has sky-rocketed. Before 2001, the total of world derivatives contracts levelled out at a staggering $100 *trillion* dollars. Two years later, that figure had doubled. By 2006, it had doubled again, and continued to climb *above* total world GDP.

Derivative trading is just one of numerous examples in which wealth is acquired not through goods or services, but by mathematics alone, without contributing any other tangible benefit to society. The present-day global marketplace employs some of the world's most sophisticated mathematicians, who orchestrate massive and volatile financial markets of staggering complexity.

Given the nature of the operations, it's easy to assume that manipulating numbers to acquire wealth is a product of our technological age, but it's not. It used to be called *usury*, and a common example was the deceptively simple practice of charging interest.

Interest and Usury

The concept of charging interest on loans did not appear until well into the history of money. For one thing, interest as a percentage was not always an easy concept for people to grasp or calculate, especially in the absence of decimal places. Such practices could not really flourish until enough borrowers and, more importantly, lenders were sufficiently comfortable with the math. The Romans, for example, charged rates that were often multiples of 12 to facilitate simple monthly calculations. Imagine calculating 14.8% interest using only Roman numerals!

Today, people apply the term "usury" to the practice of charging excessive interest on loans. However, this is an adjustment from its original meaning, inspired by a corresponding relaxation of the laws that address such practices. Originally the term "usury" was applied to any transaction in which money was acquired without goods or labour being exchanged, and where there was no shared risk. This included all loans bearing interest, as well as scenarios like sub-letting a rental unit at a higher rate than the original renter was paying. The act of making money was not the problem. Loans for ventures were not usury if the lender shared the risk with the borrower. For example, if a farmer

116

received capital from a money lender with the understanding that the success or loss of the crop was to be shared with the lender, then this was not usury. The loan was only considered objectionable when the interest to be paid was fixed ahead of time. In other words, if one was earning profit through math alone, then it was usury.

> Usury is the acquisition of wealth from others using only mathematics, with no risk, effort, sacrifice, or value-adding contribution. Until fairly recently, it was *always* considered unethical.

Laws banning the practice of usury are common to nearly every major religion. It seems that the idea of acquiring wealth by mere calculation was considered abhorrent almost from the moment the behaviour appeared. Philosophers such as Aristotle, and theologians such as Thomas Aquinas, wrote extensively on the subject, clearly recognizing that the natural essence of money was to be just an intermediary of exchange. Usury, or the charging of interest, violated the balance of this exchange; it amounted to double charging, since not only did the loan have to be repaid, but there was a further charge for its use.

The most hated sort of money-making, and with the greatest reason, is usury, which makes a gain out of money itself and not from the natural use of it – for money was intended merely for exchange, not for increase at interest. And this term interest, which implies the birth of money from money, is applied to the breeding of money, because the offspring resembles the parent. Wherefore of all modes of money-making, this is the most unnatural.
– Aristotle, ancient Greek philosopher

The counter-argument to this is that the lender is 'denied' the use of their money while it is out on loan. This is not a very convincing justification for charging interest for two reasons: Firstly, no one is being forced to lend money. Lenders choose to do so when they have more than they need and have no other use for it. Secondly, although the money could have been invested in something else, the opportunities are not equivalent. Wealth invested in a non-interest-bearing venture is subject to risk, whereas an interest-bearing loan is not (except for possible default, which we'll discuss in a moment). Why should anyone be paid to give away something that they will just get back? Furthermore, in the case of bank loans, the lender is not denied the use of the money because the money *did not exist* until the loan transaction was created. In other words, the bank gives the borrower what is essentially a bad cheque for the loan amount, representing money that the bank does not even have. The borrower is then tasked with creating real value that can be paid back to the bank. On top of that, the borrower must pay the bank interest for the privilege of creating wealth for the bank from nothing.

There is a more viable defence of interest charges: the risk that the borrower will not repay the loan. Under this circumstance, those who actually pay the full interest charge on their loans are also making up for the debtors who default on the repayment of their principal. The issue of non-payment is of course a very real problem, but there are still alternatives to charging interest. Secured loans, backed by collateral, remove the risk of non-payment since goods of equivalent value can be forfeited. Venture loans should share the risk and rewards, as described earlier. As for riskier unsecured loans with no collateral, if there was no easy profit in the practice, then the industry would shrink and people would also be much less likely to borrow money that they could not repay. Indeed, charging interest is a major factor in driving people into poverty in the first place, often resulting in their need to borrow more.

As a little side note, one reason mentioned earlier for the claimed necessity of economic growth is to create new wealth to pay the interest on loans. As it turns out, this is something of a cyclical argument. Economists will tell you that the ability to vary an interest rate is an important tool that financial institutions use to manage the economy and keep it growing.

Banking Alternatives

Banks are ethically no different from other publicly-traded commercial corporations. They are not behaving badly or immorally, and have no

118

inherent malice towards society. They are simply doing what *we* have programmed them to do: generate profit for their shareholders. However, financial institutions are often singled out as representing the epitome of a worldview that is based on numbers and greed. The fact that they operate exclusively in the mathematical realm, without relying on significant material resources, innovation, or energy inputs, means that the people they attract to manage their operations have a strong bias towards number-based thinking. This is why their 'value sins' of speculation and interest-charging seem so egregious, and why they are a primary target of those who wish to shift society's focus.

Let's look at another form of usury: One way of making fortunes within the current system is to leverage tiny fluctuations in currency exchange rates by executing very high volume transactions, sometimes repeatedly back and forth. This is reminiscent of my first equity purchase and sale, but instead of five thousand shares going up fifty cents each within a couple of months, a transaction might involve buying $100 million worth of a foreign currency in the morning and then selling it back that afternoon when its value goes up by 0.01% for a $10,000 profit. This is a clear example of dubiously creating wealth from nothing. Unfortunately, such practices can have devastating effects on small markets that are vulnerable to these massive shifts of value. In 1972, the economist James Tobin proposed a simple tax to discourage such dangerous and questionable speculation. The solution, now widely known as a Tobin tax, employs the very same principle used by the traders in the first place: Every currency swap would be subject to a fractional percentage taxation rate (e.g. 0.01%). This could be applied regardless of the total value of the transaction. For most normal trades, the tax would be mere pennies. For huge transactions, the total tax would be significant, making them less profitable and hence less attractive. A number of governments and financial regulatory institutions have shown renewed interest in Tobin taxes because of the role that such trading played in deepening the recent financial crisis. However, those who make their money that way continue to fight any form of currency exchange taxation.

Alas, for depositors who don't wish to perpetuate or support the current financial system, there is a frustrating lack of alternatives. Interest-free or "*riba-free*" banking currently exists in the Islamic world, but most of their dealings are merely a recast of standard practices using Qu'ran-acceptable terminology. The stock market offers a number of options for conscientious investors, including so-called "ethical funds". But what if you don't believe in feeding the growing economy at all? Where can you keep your money? You can't put it into the stock market or mutual funds. If you put it in a bank account, the bank will invest it and use the fractional reserve system to create new debt. Even if you spend it or give it all away, the recipient will still just deposit it or invest it. About the only thing you can do if you truly want to withdraw your support for this spiralling economy is to take your savings out as cash and put it in a safe place.

I propose an alternative that is better than just stuffing your savings under your mattress. I would like to see the creation of what I call *Platonic banking* (after Plato, who opposed usury on both practical and philosophical grounds). This user-owned service would be exclusively for the simple and safe storage of savings. It would not offer loans, pay interest, exchange currencies, or invest its reserves. All of the operations could easily be conducted online, without the need for any cash dealings, thereby providing all modern transaction conveniences. A small transaction fee would be necessary to cover the infrastructure development and maintenance costs, but it would likely be less than what mainstream banks charge now. Other than that, the balance of your deposits would be exactly what you could withdraw. By operating under a cooperative model, such banks would have no need for profit generation. In this age of electronic banking, the actual mechanics would be very easy to do; such capabilities are already in popular use with financial services such as ING Bank and PayPal. Unlike these services, a *Platonic bank* would be an entirely debt-free simplification of online banking, created to refrain from participation in economic growth or any form of usury. There would be no empty illusions of value conjured merely by mathematical operations.

> *Platonic banking* would offer an alternative that returns to the original function of money: a storage for wealth with no fractional reserve, no interest, no investment, and no debt.

A Platonic bank is nothing more than an online bank balance. In the early days, it would probably need a connection to a traditional bank account. To make a deposit, you would electronically transfer money from your standard account to your Platonic account, thus removing it from the balance that the old bank can use for investing or lending against. Withdrawals would be just the opposite. As the concept grows, conveniences such as auto-deposit, auto-withdrawal, and debit cards would be simple features to add on, thus virtually eliminating the need to interact with traditional financial institutions. This scheme offers no defence against inflation, but inflation would be slowed down the more people moved out of the current system. Critics might argue such a scheme could trigger another Great Depression, but I disagree. By adopting this alternate financial management system in a controlled and scalable fashion, we could manageably explore alternatives to our existing commercial relationships, and then implement them on a time line that we choose. Such a system would also allow the average citizen to demonstrate their declining acceptance of the status quo, and take back control of the planet's economic destiny.

> *There is no means of avoiding the final collapse of a boom brought about by credit expansion. The alternative is only whether the crisis should come sooner as a result of a voluntary abandonment of further credit expansion, or later as a final and total catastrophe of the currency system involved. – Ludwig Von Mises, economist (1881–1973)*

In Summary

The quintessential question of philosophy is "Why are we here?" Few of us would actually answer "to maintain economic growth", but that is certainly how we now manage our existence. Economic growth is the number one goal and priority of the developed world, trumping environmental sustainability and even democracy.

For those who cannot accept this global state of affairs, or who are alarmed by the excesses that caused our recent financial meltdown, it is tempting to blame the greed of individuals and institutions in the banking sector. However, they are not responsible for all of our financial ills. The root of the problem lies in the system itself, and its reliance on the limitlessness of numbers to create and measure value. That the über-rich of our world have so much is not greed – it is simply an inevitable consequence, a side effect of the numbers. The necessity for unrestrained economic growth is another unavoidable outcome of the system we created, as is the system's eventual failure.

The prediction of economic collapse is not like climate change science. There is no disputing the hard fact that a constantly growing economy consuming limited resources is an unsustainable paradigm. No numbers can say otherwise. There is no possible counter-argument that this is just some cycle that the planet is going through. The problem is accelerating, not only because growth is accelerating, but because much of the remaining resource value has already been 'spent'. Since most money now represents future value instead of existing value, even if we shut down growth, we would have to keep consuming just to balance the books. This is an unprecedented *value crisis*.

Here are the basic facts: The concept of constant economic growth, and the global value system it's predicated upon, are indeed going to collapse – that's unavoidable. This can happen in one of two ways: We can do our best to create workable alternatives and implement them as painlessly as possible; or, we can wait for the inevitable, when the system burns itself out by consuming everything around it, and then struggle to pick up the pieces. The first scenario might be preferable, but it is not as likely as the second. So which option will we choose? As with everything civilization has ever done, our choice will be driven by our values. The most prevalent value system among the powerful decision-makers is number-based and married to the growing economy model. Our challenge is to turn that around.

Nowadays, our financial system offers many opportunities for usury under its original definition: wealth created by math alone. By using computerized trading to move billions of dollars from one currency to another, speculators can make returns that are only a fraction of a percentage point in fractions of a second. When applied to huge sums of money, these practices result in sizable wealth for a zero contribution to society. The selling of debt and derivatives is another practice of usury, transferring obligations from one party to another while taking a profit just by being in the middle. Such transactions arguably *lower* the value of the obligations by increasing the distance between borrowers and lenders. Even if the debt system collapses, derivatives make it possible to bet against the stability of the system, allowing financial institutions to first profit from dangerous transactions that weaken the system, and then further cash-in their hedges against the system's failure. The simplest example of this added bonus is *short selling* (making a profit when a stock price falls), and there was a lot of this sort of trading in the lead up to the 2008 financial meltdown.

We urgently need alternatives that will give our world a better return in terms of value integrity and global sustainability. *Platonic banking* is one idea that would return money to its original function: a storage of existing wealth for future use, without usury and debt. In fact, a near-Platonic bank already exists: the JAK Members Bank based in Skövde, Sweden. It is a start, and hopefully the beginning of an idea whose appeal will expand as more people become disenchanted with the traditional banking system and its untenable reliance on our debt.

While there may still be growth left in the economy, I can't shake the notion that our planet is like a living organism. As with most life forms, there is an innate force that impels growth and maturation. But we have a word for growth that occurs beyond the bounds of natural control systems: cancer. If left untreated it invariably kills the host.

> *The whole profit of the issuance of money has provided the*
> *capital of the great banking business as it exists today.*
> *Starting with nothing whatever of their own, they have got*
> *the whole world into their debt irredeemably, by a trick.*
> *[...] There is nothing left now for us but to ever get deeper*
> *and deeper into debt to the banking system in order to*
> *provide the increasing amounts of money the nation*
> *requires for its expansion and growth. An honest money*
> *system is the only alternative.*
> *– Frederick Soddy, Nobel laureate (1877–1956)*

Chapter Seven

Numbers Incorporated

I had worked hard for nearly two years, for the sole purpose
of infusing life into an inanimate body. For this I had
deprived myself of rest and health. I had desired it with an
ardour that far exceeded moderation; but now that I had
finished, the beauty of the dream vanished, and breathless
horror and disgust filled my heart. Unable to endure the
aspect of the being I had created, I rushed out of the room. –
Mary Shelley, Frankenstein

IMAGINE IF A FEW HUNDRED years ago, the human race had created an entirely new alien species. Suppose it was a 'worker species', which could assimilate the intelligence of the people around it, and perform tasks that were too much for individual humans. These creatures would most certainly have proved useful in the early days of exploration and discovery. In the industrial age, we would surely have created many more of them to meet the demands of our progress.

Now let us presume that these creatures had their own unique value system, which embodied only a few of the characteristics of our own. They might share our ambition and drive, but have no need for friendship or morality, leading to a very singular purpose: to ensure their own interests above all else. Instead of dying as humans do, what if these creatures could instead grow larger and more powerful? With no human limitations, they would quickly rise above their worker status to positions of wealth and influence. Naturally, they would begin to demand significant input in matters affecting their own growth and prosperity, beginning with the same basic legal rights as humans. Over time, they would gain important influence in commerce and politics, and their value system would begin to take precedence over our own. These creatures might even begin to dominate civilization itself.

As you might already have guessed, this is not a fictitious proposition. Members of such a 'species' do in fact exist, with precisely the characteristics described above. They are called *corporations*.

For most of us, our interactions with corporations are fairly benign. We work for them, make purchases from them, and occasionally rely upon our governments to regulate them. But what happens when you step out of line with *their* needs and interests? A few years ago, I had just such an opportunity to find out. Make no mistake: Legally and financially, their power exceeds that of almost any other entity.

Business corporations are significant players on the world stage. They have a huge influence on civilization as we know it. In this chapter, we will learn more about corporations and the unique value system which they operate within – knowledge that is crucial to understanding our present day value crisis.

Business Corporations as Persons

Not long ago, I incurred the wrath of a huge corporation, well-known for laying claim to a phenomenal trademark territory in every corner of the globe. I was operating a one-person consulting practice called "Intellact" and had created a promotional website of the same name. A few years after I registered the domain, I received a letter from a legal firm representing Intel Corporation. They demanded that I immediately take down the site, change my business name, and never again use any email address that included the letters I-N-T-E-L.

A little research quickly told me that the monolithic chip maker had an equally large reputation for being obsessive and ruthless in trademark litigation. I was but one of dozens of businesses and organizations worldwide that had received such "cease-and-desist" letters from Intel's lawyers. One recipient was a charity working with Californian prison populations, calling itself "Yoga Inside". Apparently Intel saw that name as an infringement of its slogan "Intel Inside" and turned its legal might on the hapless yoga practitioners who were only trying to make a positive difference in their community.

I was even smaller than that charity, but as far as the courts were concerned, it would be a simple one-on-one dispute between two persons: a natural person (myself) and a legal person (Intel Corporation). Despite the monstrous imbalance and the practical impossibility of justice, the legal system would not have viewed Andrew Welch versus Intel as a contest between an individual and a large group. My adversary was a corporation – a single entity – which, like the creature imagined at the beginning of this chapter, had been endowed with the status of legal personhood.

This was not always the case. In the beginning, corporations were created to undertake projects that were considered too expensive or risky for individuals. They were often formed to accomplish a specific task such as building a bridge, mounting an expedition, or constructing a railroad, and their existence was tied directly to that task. Their advantage was that they drew upon the collective talents of several individuals and raised investments from multiple sources, increasing working capital and reducing individual risk. These early corporations existed only as long as their specified purpose. Once the project was completed, the corporation was dissolved.

Gradually, as the concept evolved, people realized that there were lasting benefits to be achieved by broadening the mandate of corporations and keeping them around longer. Today, there are many different kinds of corporations, ranging from single-person companies to municipalities and global conglomerates. For the purpose of our value system discussions, the kind of corporations I will generally be referring to are *publicly-traded business corporations*. Their value systems have specific characteristics that set them apart from other kinds of corporations and business ventures. Also, while there is international variation in legal concepts, American public corporations collectively exert the greatest influence on global commerce, so the legal context for this chapter is primarily American corporate law.

Before corporations, a business was just an extension of the business owner. The blacksmith was responsible for paying for all of his raw materials and reaped all of the profit (or loss) from his smithy. If shoddy workmanship caused an accident, he was on the hook. Corporations, on the other hand, were designed to operate as a collective entity, separate from their owners, thus protecting them from the large liabilities inherent in bigger projects. Corporations needed to be granted the rights of property ownership and the ability to enter into contracts. As a natural consequence of enforcing the contracts they entered into, they could also sue and be sued. Since the laws governing such rights were already well-defined for citizens, and the legal interactions could easily be between humans and corporations, it made sense to apply the same laws all around. Thus, a corporation was considered to be just like a person with respect to ownership and contract laws. Corporations became known as *legal persons*.

In 1886, a curious thing happened that dramatically altered the social paradigm. The Southern Pacific Railroad Corporation took Santa Clara County and the State of California to the Supreme Court to challenge a taxation law. Eighteen years earlier, the United States had ratified the Fourteenth Amendment, extending citizenship to former black slaves and ensuring equal protection under the law to all *persons*. Since the concept of corporations as *legal persons* was already widely accepted, lawyers began to argue that the Fourteenth Amendment should apply to corporations as well.

Chief Justice Morrison R. Waite, in the preamble to his decision in the case, was quite specific in stating that the amendment was *not* to be the basis for the court's decision. In that preamble, which was not part of the legal opinion and therefore carried no formal legal precedent, a court reporter quoted him as saying: *"The court does not wish to hear argument on the question whether the provision in the Fourteenth Amendment to the Constitution, which forbids a State to deny to any person within its jurisdiction the equal protection of the laws, applies to these corporations. We are all of the opinion that it does."* The original intent of the Fourteenth Amendment was clearly to confer basic human rights on freed slaves. But those last nine words, quoted out of context, were the crack that opened the floodgates. Of the 307 cases brought before the courts between 1890 and 1910 under the Fourteenth Amendment, 288 were filed by corporations, while only 19 were filed by African-Americans.

Soon corporations were using centuries-old laws with phrases like "Every *person* shall…" to lay claim to all kinds of privileges originally intended for human citizens: for example, turning our right to freedom of speech into their right to spend unlimited funds on election advertising, and even claiming freedom of religious belief to allow denial of services. Today, corporations vigorously participate in our social and political systems, but their value systems are nothing like our own.

Corporate Value Systems

Normally, when a number of individuals get together to form a group, a collective *group value system* emerges, based on the personal values of the members. While these values can't be a perfect match for all, there has to be sufficient compatibility for the group to stay together and act as one coherent entity. So a group value system can be likened to the common *human values* of its members.

Conversely, publicly-traded business corporations are not just groups of people, but rather can be considered a socially *separate species*, which has risen above our own station on the economic food chain. This is a bold assertion. After all, isn't a corporation simply one of several ways to define a group of people? They have by-laws and common goals, suggesting that their value system is just another example of a group value system – indeed a human-based value system. But this is clearly not the case. Corporations have a unifying, identifiable culture with characteristic behaviours that are different from our own. And that difference is based on the following considerations:

1. By definition, corporations are entities distinct from the humans that form them. The concept of 'legal personhood' makes them not a group of individuals but one legal individual. The implications of this go beyond mere legal formality.

2. The core of the commercial corporate value system is legally imposed upon corporations, not derived from their members. By legal precedent, a publicly-traded corporation is *required* to put the best interests (interpreted by default as the *financial interests*) of its shareholders above all else.

3. The value system of a group of people is derived from individual members, who typically exert some influence on the

decisions of the group, even at the level of nationhood. The
structure of most business corporations, on the other hand,
effectively eliminates that influence.

To better understand the difference, let's compare corporations with
societal groups that do have group value systems, such as communities
and religious congregations. People in communities are concerned
about the physical and social well-being of where they live, and their
participation in the group might include daily-life involvement, volun-
teerism, voting, etc. Members of a religious group gather for spiritual
enrichment, and participate through personal observance, communal
worship, and other collective activities. The purpose of both group
types is directly tied to human values and needs. Their objectives can
only be achieved by personal engagement. By contrast, shareholders
of publicly-traded corporations 'join' for a profitable return on their
monetary investment. For the vast majority, that is the extent of their
participation. Despite the fact that corporations are devised, created,
empowered, and run by humans to interact with humans, and have even
been given many of the same legal rights and privileges as humans,
their roots are firmly entrenched in commerce – their single value
system is monetary. They are not encumbered by the vagaries and
paradoxes of human values.

> *There is one and only one responsibility of business - to use*
> *its resources and engage in activities designed to increase*
> *its profits so long as it stays within the rules of the game.*
> *– Milton Friedman, economist (1912–2006)*

The value system of anything, from a human being to a multinational
corporation, is most easily evidenced by the decisions it makes. Making
decisions is, after all, what value systems are there to support. The
decision-making structure of publicly-traded corporations is interesting
in that the value systems of the owners (shareholders) are very rarely,
if ever, accessed. Presuming that you became a shareholder when your
financial advisor invested your money in a mutual fund, can you name
any of those corporations? Have you ever been asked for your opinion
on their policies? I'm guessing not. Operational decisions are made by

management, who ultimately report to a board of directors, who in turn are tasked with maximizing shareholder profit. Even though the board technically reports to the shareholders, it is not generally possible to have that crowd participate in any decisions. So long as the profits are acceptable, the board is usually left to do its business.

Since the corporate value system is legally mandated as a monetary one, publicly-traded corporations operate entirely under a number-based value system. The fact that they are compelled to consider the financial interests of their shareholders first and foremost, *even above the public good*, is simply the legal acknowledgement of what is already an integral part of their value system: Money is more important than anything else, and more money is better.

> Publicly-traded corporations are a *separate social species.* They make independent decisions, operate under a distinct value system, and exhibit their own characteristic behaviours.

Joel Bakan, author of The Corporation (2004), takes this one step further, proposing that if corporations were human, they would be classed as psychopaths. He lists such traits as manipulative behaviours, obsessive qualities, grandiosity, a lack of empathy, asocial tendencies, and inability to feel remorse.

> *As a psychopathic creature, the corporation can neither recognize nor act upon moral reasons to refrain from harming others. Nothing in its legal makeup limits what it can do to others in pursuit of its selfish ends, and it is compelled to cause harm when the benefits of doing so outweigh the costs. – Joel Bakan, The Corporation*

Given my claim of a distinct corporate value system, I urge caution when judging corporations harshly against human values, which Bakan seems to be doing. While they may indeed have psychopathic traits, we have to recognize that their value system (the one *we* assigned them) gives them few alternatives. In the same way, a feeding shark is not malevolent – it's just doing what it's programmed to do. Corporations are programmed to generate profit. Despite their 'legal personhood', corporations are not citizens, and not subject to human value systems.

This is not an excuse for blatant violations of rules by the corporate elite. Indeed, the argument that corporations can act independently from those who run them has sometimes been introduced by top management as an attempt to shirk personal responsibility for corporate misdeeds. As part of a landmark 1915 corporate liability decision in Great Britain, the Lord Chancellor, Lord Haldane, said in response to such ploys:

> *A corporation is an abstraction. It has no mind of its own any more than it has a body of its own; its active and directing will must consequently be sought in the person of somebody who is really the directing mind and will of the corporation, the very ego and centre of the personality of the corporation.*

While this assessment might be necessary to prosecute directors whose businesses break the law, these "abstractions with no minds of their own" do exhibit remarkably predictable behaviours, as Bakan observed. Could it be that corporations have needs and motivations unique to their legal mandate and structure? I believe the answer is yes, and I propose a new model for trying to understand what compels corporations to act the way they do.

Maslow Incorporated

In Chapter Four, we looked at Abraham Maslow's hierarchy of human needs, a model that helps us understand some of the driving forces behind human behaviour. Obviously Maslow's categories cannot be applied to corporations. Still, it is possible to come up with a different series of levels that would describe the hierarchical needs of most publicly-traded corporations. I have created a first pass of what those levels might be:

Level One

The bottom level needs for humans are *Physiological* (water, sleep, food, breathing, sex, excretion, etc.). These are all biological imperatives; without any one of them, we either die in a matter of days, or at the very least produce no offspring.

The equivalent need for the publicly-traded corporation must surely be sufficient *Revenue*. Without income or savings, the corporation will not be able to meet its legal obligations to pay its bills and staff, and protect the financial interests of its shareholders. Since it only exists as a legal entity, if it can't meet

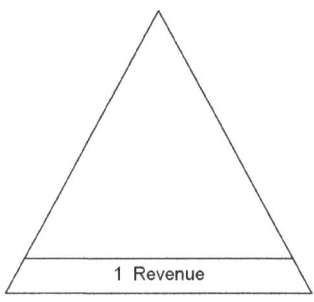

these obligations, it will die. Revenue might come from sales income, borrowed capital, or increased investment – any of these could keep a corporation alive. In the same way that a person can be put on life-support, an ailing corporation might be able to lose money for several years without folding, but ultimately, running at a loss only prolongs the inevitable: no revenue, no corporation. Like its human counterpart, the need for revenue is basic and ongoing. So long as this need is satisfied, the corporation will be motivated to pursue needs at the next level.

Level Two

The second level from the original model is *Safety* (security of property, employment, resources, body, family, health, etc.). Level two needs are primarily about protecting the individual's ability to continue to meet the needs at level one.

The equivalent in the corporate world is *Profitable Growth*. A business that is not growing or earning a profit is not going to attract investors, and is not likely to have a long lifespan. The first priority for shareholders, after profit-ability, is almost always growth. This is because their reason for buying shares is

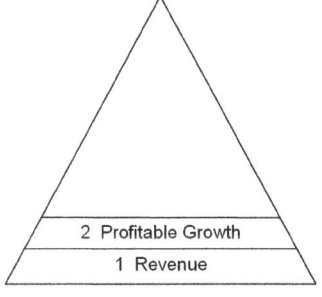

invariably to see their capital investment increase in value. Growth can occur in many forms: increases in profitability, assets, market share, sales, or perceived financial value, all of which increase the ability to

133

generate revenue in the future. Growth can also take the form of private corporations going public, opening franchises or expanding retail outlets, acquiring other businesses, or expanding services.

Most businesses have an innate drive for growth, but as with the original hierarchy of human needs, if level one needs are not being met, then the focus will quickly switch back from growth to basic survival.

Level Three

Level three of Maslow's pyramid refers to our social needs of *Love and Belonging* (friendship, family, sexual intimacy). Humans need a sense of belonging and acceptance, whether in a large group or from small social connections. In the absence of these elements, most people become susceptible to loneliness, social anxiety, and depression.

Corporations also need acceptance, not for emotional reasons, but to allow growth and profitability to continue and flourish. This level on the corporate model might be called *Public Image*. Items making up this need include brand recognition, public perception, advertising, popularity, and public sector influence. Corporations do not operate

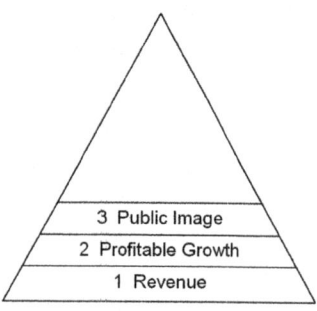

in a vacuum; at varying times they need the support of consumers, communities, and law-makers. A corporation that is profitable and growing can therefore turn its attention to its public image, investing in advertising campaigns, brand marketing, sponsorships, and industry lobby groups. While these obviously help efforts at the bottom two levels, projecting a positive image has its own distinct motivation. Employees and leadership need other people to like the company that they work for, which also feeds into the next level to be discussed.

Level Four

Maslow said that once the first three levels have been satisfied, there is an innate drive to seek the satisfaction of *Esteem* (self-esteem, respect from others, confidence, achievement). So what need does a profitable, growing, publicly-accepted corporation address next?

I suspect it will most often be *Work-force Satisfaction*. Employees are the people most intimately involved with the work of the corporation. If the workforce is not happy, the corporation will not be happy; and while it's conceivable for a corporation to remain profitable and even project a positive public image

in such circumstances, it is difficult to maintain that state. Low workforce satisfaction results in high employee turnover, low productivity, strikes, or other costly outcomes, all of which have a direct impact on revenue.

It is important to note that actions can simultaneously impact multiple levels of the pyramid. For example, a new company which is not yet profitable or growing may decide that a satisfied workforce is a high priority, and focus on actions for that. If this strategy is also a means to increased revenue, thereby addressing the primary need, then the organization can survive. It is not that Workforce Satisfaction can only be achieved after Profitable Growth and Public Image are in place; the proposed model simply states that focusing on level four to the detriment of the preceding three levels is uncommon and risky business.

Level Five

The highest level of the traditional pyramid of is Self-Actualization (morality, creativity, spontaneity, lack of prejudice, etc.). Self-actualization is the instinctual need of humans to make the most of their abilities. In short, it is the reaching of one's fullest potential.

For corporations, I propose that the highest level will be *Leadership Values*. If (and only if) every other need has been satisfied, the corporate leadership has the luxury to pursue what is important to them, and to guide their organization towards representing what they themselves stand for. This is the first possibility for human values to be

truly asserted in a corporate structure. Unfortunately, the leader values being expressed are very often just copies of the corporate values that got the leader into that position in the first place. (We will discuss leadership limitations more in the next section.)

Many assume that CEOs control the corporation and can dictate or steer its values. This can *only* be done successfully when all preceding levels of need have been satisfied. Maslow postulated that most individuals cannot effectively seek self-actualization when they still have unmet needs at lower levels. In the same way, a corporation cannot be driven by the leadership's ethical values unless the organization is profitable and growing, with a good public image, and a stable, content workforce. The only exception is if the pursuit of those leadership values will coincidentally and rapidly meet all of those lower-level needs. Just as a human pursuing self-actualization still has to eat, profitable revenue is a constant corporate necessity, and any leadership values that pose a threat to that income stream will soon be dropped when focus has to revert back to level one.

The diagram below summarizes our new model – a Hierarchy of Corporate Needs.

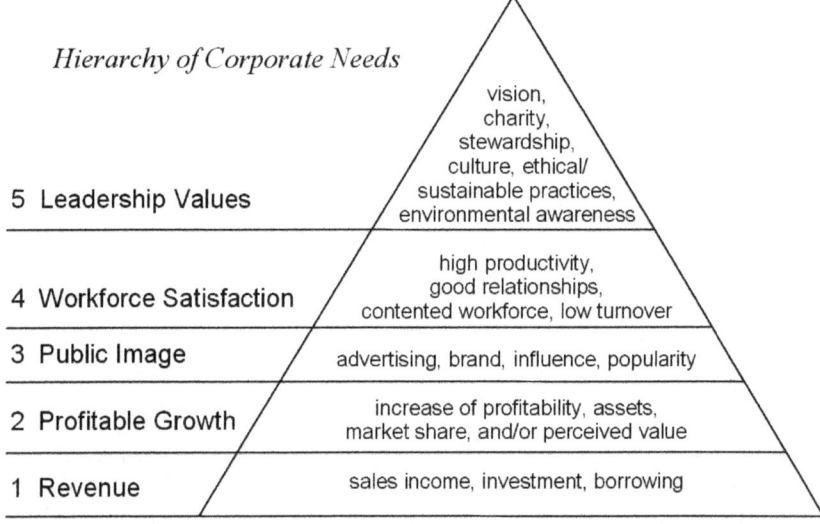

Hierarchy of Corporate Needs

5 Leadership Values — vision, charity, stewardship, culture, ethical/ sustainable practices, environmental awareness

4 Workforce Satisfaction — high productivity, good relationships, contented workforce, low turnover

3 Public Image — advertising, brand, influence, popularity

2 Profitable Growth — increase of profitability, assets, market share, and/or perceived value

1 Revenue — sales income, investment, borrowing

It is worth reiterating that this model is based on *publicly-traded* corporations. Regardless of the guiding principles of the business or the ethics of its culture, leadership must still theoretically answer to the shareholders. If we shift our focus towards privately held corporations and proprietorships, we will increasingly see organizations whose values naturally take on more of the qualities of the people who run them.

Perhaps the most significant presumption in creating this model is the capacity to prioritize the needs into multiple levels. Since nearly every level has an impact on profit and revenue, some might argue that there is only *one* corporate need, not a distinct hierarchy of them. This is a direct result of the one-scale nature of monetary-value systems – any need that can be described as a number can be applied directly to the bottom line. Still, publicly-traded corporations do focus on distinct levels of operations as they mature, and these levels are hierarchically related – enough so that the Maslow parallels are applicable and we can extrapolate useful information from the model.

Implications of the Corporate Hierarchy of Needs

Caught in the Cycle

A fundamental principle of Maslow's pyramid is that as needs are satisfied at one level, we are innately motivated to pursue the next level up. Once we have sufficient food and shelter, we move on to fulfill needs of good health, friendship, and security. But this is only possible if we are able to recognize, consciously or unconsciously, that our base needs have been met. Luckily, nature provides feedback mechanisms that tell us when we have eaten enough, slept enough, and that our core is in balance. Indeed, we can do ourselves harm by exceeding those limits.

In the corporate model, the measure of sufficient "Revenue" is profoundly affected by activity at the second level: "Profitable Growth". As the corporation grows, revenue needs increase proportionally, meaning that the limit of satisfaction is a moving target. Since numeric growth has no theoretical limit, it is not possible to accurately define a satisfactory amount of growth. Businesses can therefore constantly cycle between growth and an increased need for revenue, followed by more growth. This downward dependence does not exist in natural systems. Humans do not require substantially more food or sleep based on the number of friends that they have or their level of self-esteem.

An important distinction between human and corporate needs is that businesses can get caught in a cycle of unlimited growth potential. Since there is no certain way to recognize that lower level needs are being adequately satisfied, an organization might not promote itself to higher level needs. Thus, even well-resourced corporations may focus on the upper reaches of the pyramid only haphazardly.

The Myth of the Triple Bottom Line

In 1997, John Elkington (<u>Cannibals With Forks</u>) coined the term "triple bottom line accounting", which he defined as expanding the traditional company reporting framework to take into account environmental and social performance in addition to financial performance. The idea is that corporate social responsibility and environmental sustainability should be measured and evaluated like the financial bottom line, and should be equally important indicators of corporate health and success.

While these are indeed important principles, and may become a prerequisite for doing business in the twenty-first century, the term "triple bottom line" is misleading. For a corporation, there can only be one bottom line: *profit*. Businesses in the new age that ignore environmental and social performance may perhaps be doomed, but that is only because doing so might affect their popular acceptance and thus their financial performance. If a corporation can somehow disguise the fact that it is being environmentally or socially irresponsible, it might survive indefinitely. On the other hand, as the collapses of Enron and Worldcom show us, financial losses can only be hidden for a few years at most. The math catches up and the need at the bottom of the pyramid cannot be disguised. (Enron is a particularly poignant example, since for a long time it claimed a very high rating on its *social responsibility* 'bottom line'.)

An apt criticism to the triple bottom line phenomenon was presented by Wayne Norman and Chris MacDonald in an article in <u>Business Ethics Quarterly</u> (April 2004). They argued that, according to the proposed accounting methodology (but notably absent in the practice), the three bottom lines are supposed to be equivalently calculable – that is, they must each be reducible to a single number. But how do you accurately and objectively quantify equal-opportunity hiring practices? How do you calculate the precise value to the environment of better waste management? It is just not possible to define standard and universally-accepted units that allow social or environmental practices to be reported as a single, numeric bottom line. This is yet another example of how qualitative and quantitative value concepts do not mix.

The Hierarchy of Corporate Needs offers a more realistic model, as it allows for different values to be expressed at different levels. A manufacturer focusing on its public image might be very proactive on environmental issues. A business that is trying to increase workforce satisfaction might take positive steps in social performance. However, strictly speaking, these are not bottom-line concerns until revenue is affected. For a CEO to treat them as such would actually be a violation of the trust placed in that office by the investors.

Environmental Friendliness on the Pyramid

Care for the environment and sustainable business practices almost always entail an increase in operating costs and/or reduced production efficiency. The fact is that most businesses generate waste or by-products, and any costs associated with zero-impact handling of these wastes involve a direct reduction of ongoing revenue. Even studies to merely identify the environmental impact of operations will detract from the bottom line. Until a sufficient proportion of consumers began demanding environmentally-friendly products and practices, there was virtually no incentive for corporations to give their impact a second thought. Now, conscientious consumers have created a market that offers potential rewards for corporations that go 'green'. Sustainable practices have become a marketing issue, allowing this positive trend to be justified within the hierarchy of corporate needs.

While this is good news for the environment, it should *not* be seen as a change in corporate values. Using increased sales (or, in rare cases, cost-savings) as a means to persuade companies to act in an environ-mentally responsible manner may be the only option within corporate circles. However, it can also reinforce the false importance of money as the only value scale that matters outside those circles. Choices between promoting the environment and promoting the economy are not always mutually exclusive; but the values behind each decision are completely different and usually at odds. So while concerned citizens may applaud changes in corporate behaviour, it remains necessary to challenge the values behind them. Still, this growing trend of environmental awareness gives corporate leadership something to consider when formulating new visions and stewardship responsibilities for organizations at level five.

Limitations of Leadership

When a corporation has reached level five and is able to espouse the human values of its leadership, it is in the best position to work to the social and ecological benefit of the people it affects. Alas, even at this level, widely beneficial outcomes are not guaranteed, nor even very likely. Since the corporate value system rewards behaviours consistent with its monetary values, only the employees who embrace them will be promoted to the highest leadership levels. It would be the rare CEO who applies a radically different value system when the opportunity finally arises to take more actions for the common good.

According to the operating principles of the pyramid, after a corporation goes public, even well-intentioned leaders cannot act according to their personal values unless the needs of the preceding levels are satisfied. According to the rule of law, even organizations operating at level five cannot ignore the profit demands of their shareholders. Anita Roddick, the founder of The Body Shop, is an example of a CEO who created her retail chain specifically to espouse principal human values. Over time, the natural corporate motivation towards "Profitable Growth" motivated The Body Shop to go public. Roddick was soon caught by the conflicting legal prerogative of a public corporation, and was called to task when she started putting ethical concerns above the profits of her shareholders. She eventually had to sell the business, and the founding values faded into the background, except as marketing devices.

Before too harshly judging the behaviours of corporate leaders, one must always take into account the limitations imposed upon them by the needs and legal mandate of the corporate structure itself.

Benefit Corporations

During the writing of this book, a new kind of for-profit business corporation emerged in North America called a *benefit corporation* or *B corporation*. This intriguing variation on the corporation's traditional profit-maximizing mandate gives the board of directors legal leeway to also consider the social and environmental aspects of their decisions. The business is still subject to the hierarchy we introduced in this chapter – revenue is necessary for any commercial existence, but now the decision-makers can define parameters for how much profit is "enough", so that non-numeric human values may be brought into play.

Benefit corporations are not based solely on number-based values, since their leaders may now decide that more profit is not necessarily better, and make choices that benefit the community and environment around them. The complication is that such choices are often more difficult to make and to defend when they are challenged, but this is a good struggle to take on, and I applaud the concept.

In Summary

In the wake of globalization and free trade, many books were written that took direct aim at multinational corporations as being the cause of great ills. It is not the intention of this book to fire off more rounds at business conglomerates for profit-based misdeeds against humanity or the environment. I focus here on publicly-traded corporations, not because of their history or immorality, but because they represent a unique entity when discussing numeric versus human value systems. Corporations, existing in legal 'personhood', are the embodiment of monetary values, in direct contrast to the humans all around them.

Business corporations represent the epitome of value systems driven by numbers. Naturally, the people who invest in, work for, and lead these operations are strongly influenced by those value systems as well. However, as individuals, we can also embrace human value systems. The catch is that corporate decision-makers have a strong tendency to act using the value system of the corporation, not their own. In many cases, this is a legal and/or commercial imperative. And so the actions of corporations tend to follow characteristic behaviours and motivations as described in the Hierarchy of Corporate Needs.

The creation of an entirely new model was a daunting undertaking for someone whose formal credentials in this field are limited. I don't pretend that the model outlined in this chapter arose from significant research, nor has it been subjected to any manner of formal testing. I leave its trials and probable adjustment to those in the academic world who are better suited to the task. However, I do believe that the model makes sense on a fundamental level, and that this or a similar model can be as justifiably applied to publicly-traded corporations as Maslow's can be to individuals. In other words, I propose that the constraints on corporate behaviour, motivations, and needs are just as definable and predictable as those for humans, if not more so.

Such a model provides a very useful perspective on the 'creatures' that hold such a powerful and influential position in our global society today. It helps explain why some corporations are able to do more for society than others. It also gives us a better measure of which corporations *should* be doing more. If a corporation is profitable and growing, with a good public image, then it should be actively improving workforce satisfaction. If its revenue stream is interrupted, then we can expect the corporation to return to level one, and should not fault its leaders for focusing on that mandate.

Finally, if we can accept that a publicly-traded corporation is more than just a group of people – that it is indeed a unique 'species' with a value system quite separate from the people it employs, then we can understand that its needs and motivations are not the same as ours. The goals of corporations and those of society might sometimes coincide. However, in times of crisis, these immensely powerful legal persons will be forced to return to their mathematical precepts, putting them very much at odds with their human counterparts. It's sobering to think that even though corporations are creations of society, their power may now exceed our capacity to make meaningful changes to their status, or to revoke claims of rights unintended for them. On the other hand, that power is based on an economic structure that may itself be destined for collapse. Meanwhile, human values can still achieve small victories...

Looking back on my unintentional brush with legal annihilation, my claim to a catchy name for my consultancy seemed doomed. Intel spends more on their trademark litigation team in one year than I have earned in my lifetime; there is no way that most of their targets can afford the price of civil justice. I know only too well that had I fought back, I would have been crushed like a bug. Fortunately it never got to that point. Instead of taking on the corporation, I decided to appeal to the rational side of their lawyer – an entity who might still have a sense of proportion and propriety. Perhaps I caved enough that she could save face, or maybe she realized that I was more trouble than I was worth. Whatever it was, I survived, kept my website and email addresses, and got the action withdrawn. Thank goodness corporations still sometimes have humans to represent them.

> *I believe the mistake that a lot of people make when they think about corporations, is they think corporations are like us. They think they have feelings, they have politics, they have belief systems. They really only have one thing: the bottom line - how to make as much money as they can in any given quarter. That's it.*
> *– Michael Moore, American activist*

Chapter Eight

Numbering Our Days

Although gold dust is precious, when it gets in your eyes it
obstructs your vision.
– Hsi-Tang Chih Tsang, renowned Zen master (735–814)

IN 1999, I WAS HIRED by a new commercial theatre company to design their inaugural production for a beautiful, full-sized theatre. After 15 years of doing lighting and set design semi-professionally for community theatre, this was my first job in which everyone else was paid too. Coincidentally, around the same time, an amateur Toronto company asked me to design a production staged in their extremely challenging basement venue. While the second project was non-paying, with all volunteers, their master carpenter was also a set builder for a television series and their production values were very high. I decided to take on both projects concurrently.

With great enthusiasm, I presented designs to each theatre within a week of one other. Perhaps because of that timing, the contrast in how they were received was memorable. I gave the amateur theatre my plans for an ambitiously complex set with massive pieces on wheels, intended to portray a two-storey house – all this on a stage with an 8-foot ceiling that had the floor space of two cube vans. They loved the concept and couldn't wait to get started. My favourite quote came from the carpenter: "If you don't like any of the Home Depot baseboard patterns, let us know, and we'll custom router something that you prefer." For the remainder of that production, I felt valued, supported, and engaged.

The design for the professional company was much more basic, calling for a simple office in Act 1 that converted to a different office in

Act 2. That design was also well-received… until it got to the producer. Suddenly money was everything. The presence of flats for walls meant that someone would have to be paid to build and paint them. Every element of the set was examined for its impact on expense, not for its artistic merit. The ultimate result was not inspired. It just so happened that this commercial group didn't have a second season.

Both companies had tight budgets, and both existed to produce quality theatre. So why were the outcomes so fundamentally different? The answer lies in the value systems in play at each enterprise. When money became the chief consideration, everything changed. The attitudes were different, the level of engagement was different, and the artistic results were different too. It was a lesson that I never forgot.

This chapter explores how money changes our relationships to each other and to the world around us. While such changes might be inevitable, money and higher human values do not have to be an either/or proposition. By restoring a natural equilibrium between our value systems, we have the power to get the balance right, not just personally, but on a truly global scale.

Money… at a Cost

From basic economic principles, all else being equal, I should have derived more satisfaction from my paid theatre job than from the non-paying gig. Yet that was not the case. By changing the value system, the end results were qualitatively different, and not in the manner that one might expect. This dynamic plays out all the time in our society. Here is another example, this time with money as a deterrence instead of a reward.

In the same year as my theatre engagements, Uri Gneezy and Aldo Rustichini, two economists at the University of Chicago, were researching a problem faced by ten daycare centres in Haifa, Israel. The issue was parents coming late to pick up their children at the end of the day. Whenever this happened, a teacher had to stay until every last child had been collected. A survey showed that on average about 20 percent of the parents were late for each daycare centre. It is a widely accepted theory that if you want to reduce the incidents of a particular behaviour, you penalize the offending individual when the behaviour occurs. So the economists decided to introduce a fine at six of the ten centres. Any parent who was more than ten minutes late to pick up their child would be fined about $3 per child per incident. Sure enough the behaviour immediately changed. Late pick-ups went up – yes, up – at all six centres, every week, until they stabilized at between double and triple the previous averages. Why the unexpected result?

What the existing theories had failed to predict is that adding the fine completely redefined the relationship between the centres and the parents. Previously, the constraints on behaviour were social in nature, and the value system was one of courtesy and respect for the teachers' time – human values. Once the centres announced the penalty, the relationship shifted to a financial one. Within the new number-based value system, parents decided that the fine was good value for the convenience of arriving later, and they gratefully took advantage of this new, guilt-free option.

Perhaps even more interesting is what happened when the fines were removed three months later: Nothing changed! Once the culture of courtesy and respect had been broken, it stayed broken, and the parents continued to take advantage of the new convenience, now with no penalty. In the words of the economists: "Once a commodity, always a commodity." The human motivations and the economic motivations were incompatible, and could not be used interchangeably. Indeed, the introduction of a number-based value system, even temporarily, resulted in a permanently altered parent/staff relationship.

> The introduction of *money* in human interactions often results in behaviours and outcomes which run contrary to our established human values.

It's easy to come up with your own examples of this value shift happening. How many pleasant interactions are changed when a payment or cost is introduced? How often are political ethics compromised when there is an opportunity for easy wealth? How many business people feel forced to operate against certain social values when compelled to consider the factors of expense and profit? We bump up against the results of these decisions all the time.

> *[Money] transforms fidelity into infidelity, love into hate,*
> *hate into love, virtue into vice, vice into virtue, servant into*
> *master, master into servant, idiocy into intelligence, and*
> *intelligence into idiocy. [It is] the confounding and*
> *confusing of all natural and human qualities. ... It makes*
> *contradictions embrace. – Karl Marx, German philosopher*
> *and revolutionary socialist (1818–83)*

Unhealthy Choices

If you fly a lot, you may have noticed a trend several years ago. Once you were in the air, the flight attendant would hand out a set of small headphones to each passenger. These headphones had robust little connectors, insulated wires, and complex little ear pieces with delicate speakers that were hand-assembled with two small foam covers for the ears. At the end of the flight, these headphones were collected and tossed into the garbage after an hour or two of use. Consider the number of headphones 'consumed' for every flight, the volume of wire and plastic, and more importantly, the labour and energy used to manufacture, assemble, package, and ship each one. I can say with certainty that mathematics had determined that it cost the airlines less to throw them out than to replace the foam ear covers and reuse them. In terms of human values, this is clearly not an example of sustainable resource management, nor is there a pleasing artistry or any pride in workmanship. In fact, the practice represented a significant waste of time and materials, all destined for landfill.

In the hallways of schools throughout North America, it is very common to find vending machines for highly-sweetened, often caffeinated beverages readily accessible to the student population. Excessive consumption of such drinks is a major contributor to obesity, dental decay, and nutritional deficiencies. While parents, educators, and health professionals may be opposed to such policies, school boards are often unwilling to revise them because the contracts with the drink suppliers provide a significant source of income. Our natural instincts to protect the health of our youth are overruled in order to maintain income sources and avoid the costs of challenging the beverage companies. Even more depressing stories appear in the news on a regular basis: In India, unscrupulous doctors are still paid to amputate the limbs of perfectly healthy children and adults so that they may earn more as beggars. In Jamaica, dairy farmers dump hundreds of thousands of litres of fresh milk because they are unable to compete with subsidized milk powder imports.

> *We are most certainly the only animal that makes conscious*
> *choices that are bad for our survival as a species.*
> *– Richard Leakey, paleoanthropologist*

Single-use electronics, unhealthy products in schools, maimed beggars, dumped produce – no one believes that these choices are ultimately good for society, *not even the people who make them*. Yet these are just a few of the countless unsustainable and reckless ways that we abuse our resources and health every day. All over the world, at every level of development, decisions are made with these predictable outcomes. To simply characterize those decision-makers as greedy, careless, self-centred, or immoral is a mistake. While those elements may exist in some cases, it makes far more sense that these are just choices made using a different value system, namely the science of economics. In terms of values measured by numbers, each of the described actions is arguably the correct thing to do: The airline lowers costs, the schools increase revenue, the beggars earn more, and the market chooses powdered over fresh milk based on price.

This monetary value system is dominant because we incessantly make it so. Every single day, our news broadcast will at some point reinforce the idea of economic growth as the axiomatic goal of modern society, and we believe it. Governments everywhere direct extra-ordinary efforts in pursuit of this one objective. It drives major policies, dominates the media coverage, and is single-mindedly used as the exclusive measure of societal success. Why?

It cannot be denied that economic growth has had a significant positive impact on progress, standards of living, human satisfaction, and quality of life. Yet we need to recognize when economic growth is no longer delivering a net positive result. A nice fireplace can warm a living room on a cold night, but if you relentlessly grow the fire, you will burn down the house. The monetary value system may still provide us with positive outcomes, but these are largely short-term gains. The negative outcomes of continuous economic growth are serious and long-term, and will become impossible to ignore over time.

Furthermore, as we get used to each higher standard of living, we require ever-increasing amounts of growth to receive the same level of satisfaction. At the same time, we refuse to see or care that the immediate benefits of economic growth can be outweighed by its harmful effects. These are classic characteristics of an addiction.

> We've become *addicted* to a constantly growing economy, and to get our short-term fix, we are willing to make some very unhealthy choices.

Means versus Goals

I was recently inspired by a great talk given by Hans Rosling, a brilliant biostatistician. Rosling pointed out that when trying to understand the development of civilization, we can easily get our *means* and *goals* confused. Specifically, we are now miscasting economic growth as a *goal* of civilization, so we pursue it relentlessly. But, in Dr. Rosling's words: "Money is not a goal. It's the best mean, but I give it zero as a goal."

It's not always easy to understand the importance of distinguishing means and goals. Let us assume that individual happiness and satisfaction are commonly desired goals. If wealth can be shown to be an effective *means* to achieve these goals, then it might also be considered an *intermediate goal* – a useful rung on the ladder. But beware: It is only useful if it continues to contribute to our objective of happiness. When that's no longer the case, we have to recall our ultimate goals, and be open to casting aside any means that are no longer working.

When the economy is low and budgets are tight, governments tend to view cultural and artistic pursuits as frivolous add-ons. This is largely because culture is not seen as an effective *means* towards growth. But culture is a goal of overall human development. As Rosling points out: "Culture is the most important thing, I would say, because that's what brings joy to life. That's the value of living."

150

Questioning the assumption that economic growth is a desirable goal that consistently delivers positive social outcomes may be the single greatest challenge to resolving the value crisis that we find ourselves in. Practically every activity of the private and public sectors is based on the huge assumption that a growing economy is always a good thing. If we can even just recognize it as a powerful means instead of a goal, then we take a significant step forward. I say this because if economic growth is the means, then we must ask ourselves what our goals truly are. We have to step outside of the number-based value system, revisit our social objectives in terms of human values, and start questioning the metrics we use to evaluate the decisions we make. I firmly believe that by increasing the prevalence of human values, we can achieve *better* lives for ourselves, and also improve the prospects for our grandchildren.

Unfortunately, real change is going to take more than an adjustment of values at the individual level. We also need our governments to seriously question the notion that the well-being of civilization is indicated by economic measurements. If numbers must be used to help create policy and measure our progress, then let us use indices derived from our true goals – not ones that are exclusively and stubbornly mired in economic activity. An ideal next step would be to take a hard, critical look at the most prevalent measure of modern-day success: Gross Domestic Product.

Gross Domestic Product

The calculation of Gross Domestic Product (GDP) is used by governments the world over to measure progress and well-being. It was first introduced as Gross National Product (GNP), which is a measure of money created by and for the citizens and businesses of a given country. In the last 70 years, a rising GNP was taken to be synonymous with prosperity and growth, and it quickly assumed precedence in public policy.

As recently as 1991, this metric was widely switched to GDP, a measure economists found better suited to the exploding globalization. GDP measures the amount of money created within a country, regardless of where it goes after that. GNP/GDP maximization is now the unquestioned goal of government policy, embraced by policy-makers, academics, and media around the world. It is used ubiquitously as an indicator of a society's well-being, providing a 'score' of how well a government is doing.

The first flaw of this approach is that policies which maximize GDP are tied to the assumed desirability of economic growth. While there was a time when economic growth was directly correlated with improvements in standards of living, we now know that neither the growth nor the gains are sustainable in the long-term. And yet nearly all of society's decision-makers continue to follow policy impacts and consequences only as far as their effect on the GDP, ignoring the fact that this economic model will be unviable within a generation or two.

The second flaw of equating a rising GDP with societal improvement becomes apparent when we take a closer look at what is actually being measured. The following chart shows some of the undesirable activities that increase GDP, and some important measures that are *not* included in its calculation:

Activity measures *adding* to GDP	Value measures *not* included
• Health costs of treating those made ill through industrial processes	• Hours of labour devoted to amateur pursuits, unpaid work, and volunteerism
• Costs of civil suits as well as finding, arresting, convicting, and incarcerating criminals	• Number of unemployed persons seeking work, or homeless people seeking shelter
• Value of all species hunted to extinction and sold, such as whales, tigers, tuna, etc.	• Diminishing value of all the planet's remaining unexploited resources
• Emergency response, insurance, and medical costs of car accidents	• Level of physical/mental health, and life satisfaction of the population
• Cost of weapons used to kill people and destroy infrastructure in regional conflicts	• Proportion of wealth created strictly as a consequence of people acquiring debt

- Costs of replacing infrastructure destroyed by
  conflicts and eco-disasters

- Widening discrepancies
  between the nation's
  richest and poorest people

While the wealth-producing activities measured by GDP certainly contribute to someone's higher standard of living somewhere, it is clear that this measurement has serious limitations. The GDP is 'improved' by some very negative activities and does not reflect other measures that have an equally significant impact on our quality of life. As a monetary-value-biased index, the GDP disregards whether its economic factors are working towards humanity's betterment or not. Key determinants of how well a civilization is doing are simply ignored.

In the mid-1990s, some economists began defining alternatives to the GDP as a measurement of progress and well-being. These alternatives were still number-based (they were drafted by economists after all), but the new metrics attempted to reflect the fact that some economic activities, such as those in the left-hand column, should be *subtracted* from the total value, and that measures on the right should be taken into account. One of these new metrics is the *Genuine Progress Indicator* (GPI). While the GDP of most developed nations has risen year after year, the GPI peaked somewhere in the mid-1970s and is now on a downward trend. In other words, our countries are producing more and more wealth, while our populations are, on average, worse off and less satisfied with each passing year.

What if we had changed the scorecard of our governmental policies a few decades ago? Would it have made a difference? As it turns out, we don't have to speculate too much, since we have an actual case study to look at. In 1972, Jigme Singye Wangchuck inherited the throne to the Kingdom of Bhutan, a small country of about 700,000 people just east of Nepal. His first task, at 16 years of age, was to modernize his country. He rejected the GDP as being incompatible with Bhutan's predominantly Buddhist values, and created a new index called Gross National Happiness (GNH). Unlike the GPI, Bhutan's GNH is a policy guide for governmental actions, not a rigid mathematical measurement. It has four pillars in its counter-current approach: Sustainable Development, Environmental Protection, Cultural Preservation, and Good

Governance. While Bhutan's economy and diversity-tolerance are not perfect, the results have been impressive and profoundly relevant: Since instituting GNH as its primary goal, Bhutan has pulled itself out of abject poverty without negatively exploiting its natural resources. In a 2007 University of Leicester study, Bhutan ranked a very impressive 8th out of 178 countries for Social Well-Being, and is now one of the top 20 'happiest' countries, despite having a very low GDP.

Initiatives like Gross National Happiness are not limited to small Asian countries. Provincial, state, and national governments in New Zealand, Canada, the United States, and Australia, to name a few, have either instituted similar reporting (alongside GDP), or have at least started work on defining these new indices. They are known variously as the Genuine Progress Indicator, Social Wellness Index, Genuine Wealth Index, Index of Wellbeing, and Quality of Life Indicators.

Alas, genuine progress on the development and implementation of these metrics has been disappointingly slow. Not surprisingly, when factors start to leave the realm of monetary evaluation, it becomes difficult to find agreement on what numbers should be included. Politicians fear that the new scales will introduce biases that might favour one party platform over another. This is indicative of their reliance on numerical scores as objective evidence of why they deserve to stay in power. Mind you, most people would be alarmed at how much self-serving manipulation and redefining now takes place with 'objective' indicators like the GDP. Today's GDP is not calculated in the same way as it was in the past. In tough economic times, governments choose to compare apples to oranges, since anything else would result in an embarrassing score of their performance.

Critics of measuring well-being instead of economic growth need to be reminded that the purpose is not to develop a fairer scorecard. The aim is to totally revise the basis of government policy, so that we no longer encourage undesirable activity and instead begin to promote *genuine wealth*. The intention is to measure actual progress towards our real objectives, not the activity of tools which may or may not get us there.

The wellness measured by GPI includes economic, environmental, physical, mental, workplace, social, and political factors, making it a far more comprehensive indicator of our overall health and happiness. Even if GDP could be shown to sometimes correlate well with the GPI, it could not possibly be a superior tool for evaluating the government policies which impact these factors directly. If we truly value our environment, our health, our social well-being, and our happiness, we have to give those values equal say when we make decisions and measure our success.

The Dynamics of Sustainability

One may wonder why economic growth, which has done so well for us in the past, might now be working against us. The answer begins with some basic principles of number-based value systems, namely that they are linear and limitless. In a number-based value system, if some economic growth is better than none, then more is always better than some. In other words, the value has a direction and it must always increase in the same direction.

However, limitless systems like this do not exist in nature. For one thing, they contravene the basic *laws of thermodynamics*, a point made by Nobel chemist Frederick Soddy in his book <u>Wealth, Virtual Wealth and Debt</u> (1926). Limitless systems cannot persist when they rely on limited inputs, especially when those systems demand exponential growth. To look at this problem another way, consider the following representation of three types of systems:

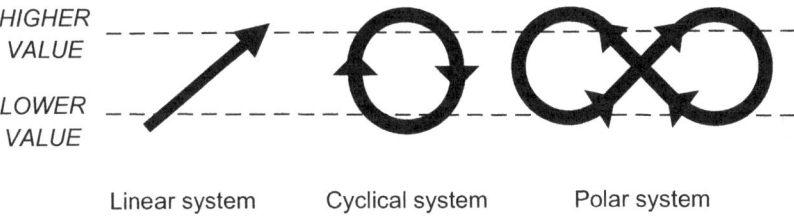

HIGHER VALUE		
LOWER VALUE		
Linear system	Cyclical system	Polar system

A *linear system* like our monetary one is unidirectional. Within such systems, there are no built-in concepts of "enough" or "too much". Any increase in input will always be of higher value, ad infinitum. In other words, there is no point at which having more money would be of lower monetary value. Linear systems therefore lack the built-in feedback loops necessary to any sustainable system.

The second type shown is a *cyclical system*. Such systems have a peak, after which 'more' yields a declining value. After the peak, the system cycles and eventually returns to a state at which more input will once again produce a higher value. Planetary rainfall is one example of a cyclical system. Plants need water, but there is a point at which they can get too much of it. Fortunately, the supply of rainwater is limited, so eventually the input will cease and the plants will begin to dry out. Meanwhile, the excess water not taken up by the plants will evaporate into the sky, where it can become rain again.

A *polar system* is one with two opposite and incompatible poles, each of which has benefits and costs. When the peak value of one pole is exceeded, the system goes into decline and then switches to the other pole in order to derive the benefits of the opposite peak. (Note the arrows in the preceding diagram.) Nature is full of polar systems, which are also known as *polarities*. For example, forest ecosystems from Australia to North America exhibit two poles of existence: rapid-growth diversity and slow-growth maturity. A forest experiencing rapid-growth diversity will become crowded, inefficient, and competitive. Eventually the most resilient and efficient species gain dominance, and the area is covered with mature growth. However, the lack of species variety and accumulation of deadwood makes mature growth susceptible to disease and fire. When calamity strikes, the area is once again cleared for the return of rapid-growth diversity.

Polarities are at the core of most natural processes; in fact, most *cyclical systems* in nature may be simplified interpretations of *polar systems*. Because the value-seeking forces within these systems are driven to constantly alternate from one pole to another, the systems cycle continuously. A key principle to grasp is that no pole is better than its opposite – each has positive and negative aspects. The only way to counteract the negative aspects of one pole is to actively seek the positive aspects of the other pole.

The survival of anything, including the human race, demands sustainability – literally, the ability of the planet to sustain our activities. Sustainability requires balance, and everywhere you look in the natural world, balance is achieved through conflicting polarities. Such systems continually cycle between two mutually exclusive states:

Death is necessary for life; monsoons must be matched with dry seasons; every inhalation needs an exhalation. Even the word "balance" can be misleading, because it can imply a static, resolved equilibrium. Polarities are conflicts that are not resolvable. Instead they are a cycle of opposites that must be traversed in equal measure. Your body never has the perfect mix of oxygen and carbon dioxide; balanced breathing is only achieved by having an excess of one followed by an excess of the other.

> Sustainability can only be achieved by recognizing and adapting to *polarities* – cycles of conflicting forces that create a dynamic equilibrium.

In order for a system to exist as a sustainable polarity, each pole must have an inherent concept of "too much" – a peak beyond which the benefits drop off and the negative consequences begin. Number-based systems have no built-in idea of "too much", so a number-based value system cannot be expressed as a polarity. But the *concept* of number-based values can be one pole of a larger value polarity, because it *is* possible to say that society has had too much of decisions based exclusively on monetary values. This is precisely the role that I see economic growth taking in our social evolution. For the last century or so, humanity has reaped enormous benefits from economic growth. Now we are passing the peak benefit of a value system dominated by financial wealth, and the negative consequences are rapidly accumulating. I propose that the value crisis itself can be framed in terms of a polarity, with human values at one pole and monetary values at the other, each with positive and negative impacts.

Exploring the Value Polarity

In his 1992 book <u>Polarity Management: Identifying and Managing Unsolvable Problems</u>, Barry Johnson outlines a useful framework for analyzing polarities in organizations. Once the two opposing poles have been identified, the next step is to separately list the positive and negative outcomes of each pole. In the quadrants below, I have listed aspects of a society dominated by human values and one dominated by monetary values:

Human Values Dominant	Monetary Values Dominant
Positive Outcomes	**Positive Outcomes**
▪ Emphasis on ethical practices ▪ Cultural diversity ▪ Long-term impact thinking ▪ Better resource management ▪ A healthier environment ▪ A human-centric approach to problems	▪ A growing economy ▪ Opportunities for affluence and prosperity ▪ Facilitated international trade ▪ Simplified decision-making ▪ Technological advances ▪ A rational, scientific approach to problems
Negative Outcomes	**Negative Outcomes**
▪ Economic depression ▪ Fewer opportunities for prosperity ▪ Trade barriers and smaller markets ▪ Tougher decision-making ▪ Fewer technological conveniences ▪ Subjective, 'irrational' thinking	▪ Resource depletion and waste ▪ Loss of cultural diversity ▪ Borrowing from the future ▪ Short-term impact thinking ▪ Unsustainable growth ▪ Environmental degradation ▪ Disparity between rich and poor

Johnson suggests that we tend to move through all polarities in a predictable cycle, as indicated by the arrows. Seeking the positive outcomes of one pole, we strive for that ideal. So if we put ourselves into the top-right quadrant, we enjoy the benefits of a monetary value system. Inevitably, as we begin to experience the negative outcomes, we sink into the problems of the bottom-right quadrant. In terms of the value crisis that I posit, this is where we are today. Eventually, we might become attracted to the positive outcomes of the opposite pole, and shift over in an attempt to solve our problems. This will indeed be a positive step. However, as is the case with all polarities, the other pole will have negative outcomes too. When those of the bottom-left quadrant become intolerable, we will shift once more and the cycle will repeat itself.

I have no doubt that this polarity of value systems exists, and can be observed on both micro and macro scales. Society has experienced all four quadrants in the past, and yet one of our greatest challenges is the fact that we neither recognize nor manage these issues as a polarity. As a result, the global pendulum has swung so far towards the pole of the monetary value system that any hint of what the other pole looks like represents a massive shift in thinking. There is no right or wrong pole in a polarity – each has its positive and negative effects. The real danger is to blindly spend too much time at one pole, preventing any natural counterbalancing.

Many visionaries and learned academics have proposed excellent strategies on how to return society's focus to human values, and thus rebalance our polarity of value systems. In Chapter Ten, we will take a look at the role that key players can take in championing the opposite side of our current pole. My objective here is to provide a framework that shows why our current systems are failing, and how a new world-view might help get us out of this value crisis and the environmental and financial crises that inevitably follow from it.

In Summary

The introduction of money turns a human experience into a transaction. In doing so, the participants instinctively switch to a monetary, number-based value system in order to determine behaviours, evaluate options, and measure resulting happiness. Incompatible values such as integrity, pride, empathy, joy, learning, and courtesy are all pushed aside. It's not surprising then that these human values have no real sway in the world of commerce. Instead, we use the math of our net gain or loss to evaluate our satisfaction and the perceived fairness of the interaction.

Unfortunately, the more we rely on the numbers, the more we lose the win-win potential of other value systems. When the only value that we use is numbers, every set of choices is ultimately a zero-sum game, and every transaction has a winner and a loser, or at best a break-even.

Since winners have more power over future transactions, it is inevitable that a small percentage of the population will emerge as super-wealthy, and so the spiral continues. Money rapidly becomes the objective instead of just a means to achieving an end.

This single-minded fixation is best exemplified by our reverence for Gross Domestic Product as the number-one indicator of progress and societal success, despite its significant flaws. Fortunately, some of the alternatives to GDP measurement are gaining ground. For instance, the Canadian House of Commons passed a bill in 2003, directing the government to develop and report on a set of social, environmental, and economic indicators of the health and well-being of the people, communities, and ecosystems in Canada. More recently, in July 2011, the United Nations unanimously passed resolution #65/309, which recognized "that the gross domestic product indicator by nature was not designed to and does not adequately reflect the happiness and well-being of people in a country", and invited "Member States to pursue the elaboration of additional measures that better capture the importance of the pursuit of happiness and well-being in development with a view to guiding their public policies." The UN has since begun the process of implementing such indices in member states around the world.

Our number-based value systems, with their limitless, linear scales, are not based in any kind of natural reality. I claim this because every process of nature is firmly rooted in balances, feedback loops, and sustainability. Unsustainable concepts become dead branches on the evolutionary tree, dropping off to make way for systems whose viability looks after itself. The more we adopt such flawed value systems as replacements for our own, the more we become tied to their fate.

To return to my opening theatre set design story, the over-the-top hours I spent in theatrical pursuits were matched only by my excessive hours working as a computer analyst. My Information Technology clients were often bemused by my commitment to this contrasting life of mostly unpaid extroverted creativity. I now realize that I was simply doing polarity management for myself. Theatre provided the artistry, passion, and celebration of achievement that was often missing among the office cubicles. While no software is ever truly complete, theatre had a closing night, and thus personal closure. On the other hand, it

160

didn't pay the bills or give me the same sense of having a practical impact. The whole concept of a good work/life balance is the idea that there are numeric and non-numeric values. What works in one realm makes no sense in the other, but we need both to have rich, fulfilling, healthy, and happy lives.

My proposition is that society itself needs a better work/life balance. We need to spend more time and energy exploring that other pole of values, which cannot be expressed in numbers. Forest ecologies depend on a cycle of *growth* and *destruction* in order to maintain a thriving diversity of flora and fauna. There is no optimal state for those biospheres. Their survival requires a repetition of the natural cycle of overgrowth, clearing, and renewal – forces that act against each other and define the polarity essential to their sustainability. Our own future and evolution depends upon such polarity management. I contend that similar forces should apply to our economic system.

> *At present we are stealing the future, selling it in the*
> *present, and calling it gross domestic product.*
> *– Paul Hawken, environmentalist*

Chapter Nine

Numbers Rule

*Democracy encourages the majority to decide things about
which the majority is ignorant. - John Simon, critic*

A S THIS BOOK WAS BEING written, an interesting juxtaposition of mass protests were being staged at home and abroad. Throughout North Africa and the Middle East, the "Arab Spring" saw hundreds of thousands of demonstrators seeking to overthrow dictators and author- itarian governments in order to give power to the people. Meanwhile, a series of much smaller protests with less-defined objectives known as the "Occupy Movement" sprang up in 95 cities across 82 developed countries. Both conflicts were international in scope and both were grassroots campaigns directed against those in power. However, the political environments in which they were created were worlds apart.

The uprisings in Tunisia, Egypt, Yemen, Libya, and Syria called for an introduction or reinstatement of *democracy* – literally "rule by the people". In contrast, the Occupy Movement emerged in the estab- lished democracies of North America, Europe, and elsewhere. Indeed, one of the Occupy Movement's battle cries was a call-and-response chant: "What does democracy look like?" "This is what democracy looks like!" So what had happened to the democracies that the Occupy protestors lived in? The general sentiment amongst the activists was that their governments were ruled by the wealthy, not by the people. They claimed that the wealthiest 1% wielded a grossly disproportionate share of the power based upon their financial resources. As part of the 99% majority, the protestors wanted to take the power back.

Majority rule is the cornerstone of our democracies. So how did it come to be that a vocal number of citizens could correctly claim that our government's democratic decisions are unduly influenced by the moneyed minority? Furthermore, decision-making by voting, being yet another number-based value system, is again limited to quantitative measurement. So does the majority of the population really have any claim to making better decisions than those who own the majority of the wealth?

In truth, there is little basis for suggesting that either group can consistently make choices with superior outcomes for all. This chapter takes a critical look at our current form of rule-by-numbers democracy, and explores what might be possible in our technologically connected world.

Governing Values

As a young student growing up in Canada, my first experience of formal participation in democratic procedure was casting a vote for the student council. Each year, beginning in Grade 7, our homeroom teacher would announce that it was time for us to nominate and elect a representative from our class. If more than one candidate was put forward, we closed our eyes in a primitive form of secret ballot and voted for our choice by a raised hand. Thus, we all experienced the first universal principle of democracy: *one person, one vote*. Whoever got the most number of votes won, giving us our second lesson in democratic principles: *majority rule*. For most of us, this was a radical departure from the power unquestionably residing with our parents, our teachers, and anyone else who had the years or muscle to enforce a dictatorial rule.

In developed countries, we tend to think of ourselves as being democratic. But in reality, we use a whole spectrum of methods to make group decisions, ranging from *autocracy* (in which the designated leader decides) to variations of *democracy* (in which everyone is consulted). Ask most school teachers how they run their classrooms and you'll soon notice an autocratic trend. In the realm of criminal justice, the legal code in Canada and most of the United States long ago rejected the idea of a jury deciding on the fate of an individual by majority rule. Instead unanimous decisions are required. Anything less than that would leave too much room for reasonable doubt.

From the beginning of the first social units, humans have wrestled with the complexities of acting as one coherent group. When group decisions need to be made, a value system is required. In a total dictatorship, the personal values of the leader might rule the day, but generally speaking the collective will develop its own *group value system*. These group values determine our laws and our social norms, as well as the methods by which we enforce them.

Of course group value systems cannot be a perfect match for all the individual values of their members. As the population increases, the number of values and priorities in common across the group will naturally decrease. Over the course of human history, sophisticated group value systems have emerged to try to address the needs of the many while respecting the values of the few. Some communities put faith in the wisdom of their leaders to ensure the collective good, while others consider the rights of the individual to be paramount. Within democracies, we employ a variety of group decision-making systems based upon the challenge at hand. Around the world, our political and social systems are even more varied.

If I could point to a common thread in the evolution of group decision-making, it is that we ultimately strive for systems that are manageable, fair, and effective. If a system fails on any one of those levels, we become embroiled in the chaos of change, from a structured re-ordering like a better voting system to a radical overthrow like the Arab Spring.

> There are three objectives for an optimal group decision-making system: *manageability*, *fairness*, and *effectiveness*.

These three important objectives – values, if you will – are difficult to measure. Manageability might be estimated by the time and cost of the decision-making process; fairness is an innately qualitative human judgement; and effectiveness is an indistinct concept encompassing the net value change to the group. The inherent challenge of getting it right is the reason why we employ so many decision-making systems around the world.

As a corporate facilitator, I have worked with many groups struggling to make better decisions, usually by including more input from individuals. The current holy grail in organizational development circles is decision-making by *consensus*, where the decision might not be everyone's choice but everyone agrees to fully support it. The key benefits are that decisions are fair (being more inclusive) and effective (with better outcomes that are well implemented). However, as the group size increases, consensus can take a lot more effort. Every vote is of equal value, but the values are not additive: a single vote of non-support can potentially suppress a decision. A consensus system can therefore present a manageability challenge.

Consensus democracy is not a new concept. In fact, in the oldest and longest-standing societies studied by social anthropologists today, decisions by consensus are the norm. Take the case of the nomadic San people of the Kalahari, one of the few hunter-gatherer societies still in existence. Their society consists of loose coalitions of open, assertively egalitarian communities known as bands. Not only is there no need for any kind of hierarchy in their group structure, but their value system actively discourages the emergence of a civil authority. Since they live in small bands whose members spend so much time in close proximity, the group value system reflects their personal value systems to a degree unknown in modern western communities. Their ties to a specific band are loose enough that if a conflict did arise, the individual(s) concerned would just split off to join another band.

Most other ancient cultures evolved from bands into the villages, states, countries, and empires that we have today. As these social units grew in size, seeking consensus would have quickly become unmanageable, and so other solutions emerged. Thus, the advent of autocracies, in which the leaders make all the decisions, and more complex political structures such as *representative democracies,* operated by majority rule.

In this book, I am more interested in exploring the representative democracies. With their multi-level reliance on numbers, these systems upon which we base our entire political framework are actually just another way that we let quantitative measurement rule over qualitative values.

Democracy by Numbers

Much of the developed world, including the planet's greatest super-power, is run by *representative democracy* – a process whereby elected individuals represent us and make decisions on our behalf. Typically, elections are decided by *majority rule*, or which politicians receive the most number of votes. Government decisions are made by the very same principle. It is therefore important for us to take a critical look at representative democracies and see how well they meet our objectives for good governance; that is, how manageable, fair, and effective they really are.

Are They Manageable?

Majority rule is an easy, quantitative way to decide on choices, and it's the most common method for including any number of people in a group decision. In its simplest form, it is certainly a very manageable system: The person or choice with the greatest number of votes wins. However, if the question involves more than two options, majority rule becomes problematic. By simply adding one more option, there is the possibility of a 40-30-30 split – a scenario in which the winner with the most votes is not the option desired by the majority. Instead, the result is *minority rule*.

In representative democracies, minority rule can be a common occurrence when there are more than two candidates in the race. To address this shortcoming, a number of countries have come up with system variations such as *preferential voting* (in which voters rank all of the candidates in the order that they support them) or *proportional representation* (in which parties gain seats in proportion to the number of votes cast for them). While such systems may be fairer, they increase the complexity of representative democracies, especially when they combine elections with appointments for proportional rebalancing.

Are They Fair?

We have already observed that majority rule can actually lead to minority rule, which is a contradiction of principles. But even in a simple yes-no decision, the fairness of majority rule can be called into serious question because it threatens the rights of minorities and the unique needs of individuals, exhibiting what is often referred to as the *tyranny of the majority*. Countering this effect is an ongoing struggle in groups of all sizes.

> *A democracy is nothing more than mob rule, where fifty-one*
> *percent of the people may take away the rights of the other*
> *forty-nine. - Thomas Jefferson,*
> *American president (1743–1826)*

In addition, special interest groups can easily target a single election campaign or elected representative to leverage significant amounts of power. In many countries, including the United States, major corporations can direct millions of dollars to support the campaigns of political candidates favourable to their profit margins. In the 2012 American federal election, just 132 people (0.000042% of the population) gave 60% of the money spent by the influential Political Action Committees (Super PACs). Such contributions compellingly influence campaigns and can shape the election outcome.

Once the elected representatives are in office, they are subject to intensive professional lobbying. Single corporations, industry groups, and small minorities can affect the outcome of a broad range of decisions, without having to sway the opinion of a majority of the people. All of this renders the system more akin to *one dollar-one vote*, and inarguably gives a few entities far more impact on societal decisions than your average citizen. Some say democracy is the best system money can buy.

Furthermore, a single election-time vote has to be applied to multiple issues. Who do you vote for if you support Candidate A's position on taxes and Candidate B's position on crime? Once the election is over, the role of the people in political decision-making is even more significantly diminished. Representatives typically hold their posts for years after they gain office, so the power of the original vote does not guarantee a specific outcome – particularly on issues that were not on the radar at election time. Constituents can participate in polls and grassroots activities, but their influence is limited and they are often out-gunned by full-time lobbyists with different agendas.

The time lag between elections and legislative decisions is even more problematic when the population has lost confidence in the government, but has no recourse until the next election. In 1988, one of the Canadian federal parties won a solid election victory, giving them 169 out of 295 seats in parliament. Five years later, the same party won just two seats. What changed? The policies? The political climate? It doesn't really matter. The point is that there was a dramatic shift in public opinion that was not reflected by the system until much later. It is safe to wager that in that government's final years, decisions were made and implemented that ran contrary to the wishes of a huge proportion of the citizens. This calls into question both the effectiveness and fairness of a model of democracy in which we only go to the polls every three to five years.

Are They Effective?

Do representative democracies produce effective results? Are the outcomes better than they would be with the alternatives? I was not yet 12 years old when I had my first classroom voting experience, but even then it was obvious that the process was a popularity contest, driven more by friendships than by any thought of effective representation. In the grown-up world of democratic elections, popularity can still take precedence over effectiveness. And yet, even if one were to rigorously research the political and intellectual merits of each candidate, what does it mean to be effectively represented? Ethical politicians have long struggled with whether to use their own best judgement on an issue, whether to vote with the will of their political party, or whether to side with their constituents. Do we vote for a candidate because we believe they will do the right thing or because we believe that they will do what we want?

Even if we can solve all of the problems above, the ability of majority rule to produce the most effective decisions relies on some very significant assumptions. Firstly, there's the requirement that the people with the best ideas will be given a forum in which to suggest their options. Secondly, there's the hope that the majority will choose to participate in the vote, be permitted to vote freely, be fully informed of the options, and ultimately vote for the best idea. A democracy is only effective if there's an open decision-making process, with informed, engaged, and rational people comprising the majority.

Democracy is the recurrent suspicion that more than half of
the people are right more than half of the time.
- E. B. White, author (1899–1985)

The probability of a well-informed citizenry making good decisions is further reduced when the voter is distant from the decision in time, location, or understanding. Imagine a scenario in which a referendum is being held to resolve a fishing rights conflict. Why should the votes of several disinterested, uninformed, unaffected, inland citizens carry the *same weight* as the vote of a fisherman directly connected to the issue, or an aquatic biologist studying the problem, or an ethicist working with the parties to find a solution? This is equivalent to asking everyone in a hospital, be they patients or staff, to vote on the new standard surgical procedures for the hospital's operating rooms.

> Majority rule results in the best decisions only
> when the population is sufficiently informed,
> interested, engaged, and consulted – typically a
> rare combination.

The inherent shortcomings of majority rule are further amplified in representative democracies by multiple layers of voting, and a wide gulf between decision-makers and the general population. And yet, in every election, we expect to get the very best decision-makers by giving everyone in the country a slate of perhaps three or four candidates to choose from. We then expect the resulting governments to make the best decisions affecting almost every aspect of our lives for the next few years. Incredible! Perhaps the best reason that the representative democratic system seems to work is that the bulk of day-to-day decisions are not made by elected officials, but by experienced public service bureaucrats who are often better suited to perform that task – autocratically. These informed and engaged professionals also spend a lot of time educating and advising our politicians so that they have a better chance of making good policy decisions.

170

When great changes occur in history, when great principles
are involved, as a rule the majority are wrong.
The minority are right.
- Eugene V. Debs, American socialist (1855–1926)

Meanwhile, there is one more tragic flaw of representative democracies – the requirement of having *professional politicians*.

Staying in Office

Popular politicians will get re-elected; unpopular politicians will not. So an extremely important side effect of a representative democracy is short-term thinking. In order to keep their jobs, politicians must make choices that will produce a positive payback within their term of office, relegating any negative consequences to the longer term. Instead of desirable societal outcomes being the top priority, there is a very strong tendency to put the goal of re-election first. As a result, decisions that produce short-term benefits with deferred costs will be favoured over those with immediate costs and a long-term payoff, even if the latter will produce a much better result for the constituency over time. Any government that 'errs' on the side of strategic, long-term policy-making will often find itself replaced by the opposition in the next election, which typically rides in on a popular wave of support to thwart and reverse those same decisions.

> Representative democracies favour decisions
> that produce short-term benefits.
> Most long-term objectives are either ignored, or
> leaders cannot stay in power long enough to
> achieve them.

Since a politician's job becomes subject to the whim of the voters every time an election rolls around, it is necessary for their decisions to be *defensible*. If a government can't defend its decisions to the masses, then the masses will cease relying on them and will change either the structure or the players. This introduces what I call a *defensibility bias* – a bias that further favours number-based values over human values,

171

since numbers can provide solid evidence that their decisions are 'correct'.

Earlier in this book, we discussed our society's discomfort with subjective decision-making. By reducing policy choices to numbers, governments can make decisions that appear rational, objective, and defensible. If politicians can claim that their proposals are driven by numeric data, they can relieve themselves of some of the responsibility for less-attractive outcomes (and when a great number of people are affected, there will always be some who are negatively impacted). That's why defending policies with "economic realities" makes political sense. Money is a value scale that everyone can understand. While opponents may not always agree with policy directions, everyone can agree that increasing a nation's financial prospects is good. Decisions based on human values are a trickier proposition, since not everyone shares the same social, cultural, or ethical perspectives.

> Representative democracies favour decisions
> that are *defensible*, which introduces another
> social bias towards number-based value systems.

Take for example the Kyoto Protocol, a major international treaty to tackle climate change, which was signed and ratified by more than 180 countries. The United States was the only major country that refused to ratify the agreement. Most of those who opposed ratification did not officially disagree with the spirit of the treaty, the science of global warming, or the moral imperatives represented by the near-unanimous planetary effort to collaborate on the problem. Instead, they defended their position primarily on the economic impacts of participating. Since it's hard to argue with the numbers, monetary value scales have become a powerful way to evaluate group options and end further debate on topics such as this one. Thus, numbers not only determine who represents us through voting, they also influence what policy choices are proposed, and how those options are evaluated. This gives number-based value systems extraordinary influence over our societal decisions.

Of course, I'm not the first person in history to recognize the limitations of an elected democratic government and what it takes to stay in power. Solutions to counteract such pitfalls are as old as democracy itself. Many political systems incorporate unelected houses of power such as senates or monarchies to provide varying combinations of *meritocracy* (rule by ability) and/or *plutocracy* (rule by wealth), as well as continuity. As a student, I was fortunate enough to be selected to join the Forum for Young Canadians, a group of about 100 youths from across the country who gathered in the nation's capital to learn more about the Canadian parliamentary system. One of our daily field trips included a tour of the office of the Speaker of the Senate, that house of parliament populated by unelected, appointed senators. A quote emblazoned on the wall stuck with me:

> *Principum munus est resistere levitati multitudinis. (It is the*
> *duty of the nobles to oppose the fickleness of the multitude.)*
> *– Cicero, Roman statesman and philosopher*

At the time, I thought this was a justification of an arbitrary power: Those with the money were expected to make the decisions for hapless have-nots. I later learned of a second Cicero quote in the same office that complements the first one:

> *Plus apud nos vera ratio valeat quam vulgi opinio. (Let*
> *reason prevail with me [us] more than popular opinion.)*

Taken together, these quotes point to the fact that for at least 2000 years, humans have in some way questioned leaving all of the power in the hands of the majority (or even, by extension, a representative democracy). I actually agree with Cicero's grand intention, that the pure strength of numbers alone should not sway all of our major decisions. The key question therefore becomes: "Whose opinion or vote should carry more weight?" While the word "nobles" has significant social class and wealth implications, there are other ways to interpret it for our modern society. Nobles might also describe people with "noble intentions" – those who selflessly become engaged in the advancement of the greater good for little or no personal gain. Could it be that such people might play a larger part in our group decision-making system, resulting in higher-value outcomes for our society? If so, how might this be achieved?

A New Take on Participatory Democracy

Decision by consensus is an age-old option that can yield superior results, but has always been impractical for a large group of citizens. It's simply not possible to hear from everyone, address each and every concern, and consistently select a one-size-fits-all solution that everyone can support. However, there may be some middle ground in yet another flavour of democracy, called *direct* or *participatory democracy*. In a participatory democracy, the people have the potential to be fully engaged at every level of the decision-making process, without representatives as stand-ins for public opinion. Until very recently, this system has not been manageable on a large scale. But in today's technological and collaborative culture, we may be able to put participatory democracy back on the table for communities of any size.

Participatory democracies give every stakeholder the opportunity to participate directly in decisions. Studies have shown that when everyone is engaged in deliberations, participatory democracies produce superior discussions, with more sympathy for opposing views, less partisanship, and greater respect for evidence-based reasoning. In other words, they produce very effective results and inspire high levels of commitment. This increases the likelihood of consensus without necessarily demanding it. There can be little doubt that such a system would be considered a fair one, since everyone in the community has equal access to participate. So the question becomes: How do we make such a system manageable? I suggest that the answer can be found in the power of the internet. Specifically, I propose a *wikiocracy* – a version of participatory democracy that uses the internet as a fundamental tool for participation.

The inspiration for this approach comes from the Wikipedia project. Wikipedia is a powerful information tool whose content emerged from and is maintained by the general population. It is a wide-ranging, ever-expanding, multilingual online encyclopedia with extensive cross-references and links to external resources. What's amazing is that anyone with internet access can add topics or edit the content. Thus it draws on the collective knowledge and viewpoints of anyone who cares to contribute. At first, it might seem that the content is vulnerable to extreme bias and vandalism (*the fickleness of the multitude*). However, thousands of volunteers worldwide constantly monitor, verify, and edit every addition and change. Many have significant expertise in the areas they watch over – truly a *noble* pursuit.

This model of open collaboration has some remarkable properties. The information (which is constantly open to further enhancement) comes from the hard work of relatively few individuals – those who care enough and take the time to create and edit the content. These people are not appointed or elected or sold that privilege, nor are they paid for their time and efforts. While the number of hard-core editors and contributors might be small (each one leaving their mark on hundreds or thousands of articles), it is still possible for one unknown person to make a significant contribution to a single article and have that remain as a lasting resource. Wikipedia is but one example of how thousands of people are working together on globally significant projects without any hierarchy of decision-makers, formal votes, externally imposed plans, or monetary compensation. Other examples include *open source* software projects such as Linux – the freely available operating system which has been challenging the exclusive supremacy of Microsoft Windows. The Wikipedia project proves that such collaboration is possible, that interested persons will put in the time and effort, and that the technology and protocols can make sense of the volume of input.

While I am not the first to coin the term *wikiocracy*, there is still no formal definition of what constitutes such a system. As a starting point, I propose the following guiding principles:

Data Gathering	In addition to the regular data gathered by professional public servants on a governance issue, anyone is able to contribute additional credible, confirmable data.
Data Access	All relevant data on a governance issue is consolidated and accessible online to everyone.
Information	Impartial interpretations of the data and additional information can be created and edited online by anyone, subject to requirements of a neutral point-of-view.

Opinions & Dialogue	Subjective opinions and constructive dialogue are possible in appropriately identified forums.
Policies & Legislation	Policies and legislation are collaboratively created and edited in open online documents.
Everyday Decisions	Day-to-day decisions, guided by existing policies and legislation, are made by professional public servants, and the results are accessible online to everyone.
Significant Decisions	Significant decisions are made by an open 'poll' of citizens to test for support, using all of the above resources. (Even a test for consensus demands a survey of some sort.) In the environment of the preceding principles, polling in a wikiocracy could avoid the pitfalls of the voting practice in a representative democracy. For example, if a proposition does not gather sufficient 'votes', it means that it has to be reworked until it does.

Let's explore how these principles address our three objectives for group decision-making.

Is a Wikiocracy Manageable?

Today's internet and social-networking technology can easily manage thousands of people collaborating on projects. Much of the data associated with community governance is already on a computer somewhere – new tools can now solve the challenge of making it findable and accessible. Websites like wikinews.org and the Wikidata project already show promise for the effective implementation of the principles outlined above.

Is a Wikiocracy Fair?

Every citizen would have full access to the process and could participate to any degree they chose – from ignoring it, to observing it, to actively contributing to it. Access would not be arbitrarily influenced by income level or personal connections. Socioeconomic factors might still play a role in internet access and time to participate. More would need to be done to level these obstacles.

Is a Wikiocracy Effective?

While every person has *potential* access, the Wikipedia model shows us that the people who will do the most work will likely be the ones with the passion, commitment, and expertise to do so. Note that these are not prerequisites: Any individual who has a positive contribution to make can have their ideas included and acknowledged.

It is not hard to see that these attributes could lead to better outcomes for the whole group. Policies and legislation would benefit from extensive input and ideas from all stakeholders. Proposals that signify larger changes from the status quo could be more extensively explored and debated, well before they are submitted to the general populace for acceptance or rejection. The bias for short-term decision-making could be alleviated by eliminating elected representatives; no longer would politicians be torn between staying in office and doing the right thing. Instead, much of their role could be added to the work of the existing public sector, where individuals work for the government profession-ally, as indeed they do now. No one would need to appeal to the population for re-election, nor would anyone be straitjacketed by party policies. Any power that could be improperly influenced would face a multitude of checks and balances.

> Modern networking technology opens up a huge potential for improved large group decision-making using participatory democracy – a *wikiocracy*.

References to a wikiocracy concept go back to at least 2005, when Iranian activist Hossein Derakhshan proposed that a review of Iran's constitution take place in an internet forum. In Iceland, such a review did in fact take place. Subsequent to the devastating effects of the 2008 financial crisis on that country, a special commission conducted a fully participatory, online revision of their constitution, and submitted it to the Icelandic parliament in July 2011. On a smaller scale, the cities of

Dallas and New York have both experimented with *wiki-policies* – openly refining legislation with the online participation of the public. While there are still numerous challenges for security, privacy, internet access, etc., further experiments with the wikiocracy concept could lead to new platforms that rethink the way we formulate policies, make decisions, and govern ourselves.

Detractors might characterize Wikipedia itself as an apparatus for the 'tyranny' of an active, engaged minority, but for all its faults, it is an extremely powerful tool. Imagine if one day society operated in this fashion. Every voice would have the potential to be heard, and every citizen would have equal access to participate, but the main contributions would come from those 'noble persons' who have the willingness, experience, and interest to contribute the most. To me, this feels as natural as consensus. By leveraging the technology, we can expand the practical group size of this decision-making system to numbers that were once unimaginable. This would restore the real goal of democracy: Giving power to the people.

In Summary

Today, most of the developed world accepts majority rule as the de facto standard for decision-making in their governments, organizations, corporations, and any other group. Alas, by evaluating important decisions solely on the basis of their polled popularity, we are once again relinquishing our power to numbers, and paying the inherent costs of those principles. Firstly, majority rule operates on the assumption that there is one best answer, which is quantifiably determinable. Secondly, it assumes that every individual is equal, so that three opinions, like three dollars, are worth the same, regardless of who voices them. But assigning greater value to an opinion just because more people support it is an incomplete strategy that's not always appropriate. When a group votes 25 "for" and 2 "against," it makes a difference to know who those two people are and what information they might have.

Relying on majority rule contributes to our value crisis because it dismisses the unquantifiable attributes that are essential to making the best decisions. While every person in a group should have an equal opportunity to participate in the discussion, there is no practical or even ethical reason why each person's opinion should be forced to carry equal weight. I don't think it inconsistent to believe that every person should be valued equally, but every person's contribution in every single case need not be.

The reality of representative democracy is that it enshrines contradictory principles. When individuals are elected to decide policies for the many, you get unequal participation in all decisions, and reduce opportunities to leverage interest, expertise, and engagement from the people who care most. The promise of majority rule also often leads to either *minority rule* or the *tyranny of the majority*. Moreover, a system that relies on paid politicians creates an inherent bias towards evaluating options and measuring success using number-based value systems, with a myopic focus on short-term benefits. The targeted influence of funded special interest groups is far more effective than the limited influence of the citizenry, which is largely restricted to election years.

In spite of its many shortcomings, much of our civilized society considers representative democracy to be the highest form of political decision-making. When flaws are pointed out in its fairness and effectiveness, or even its bias towards wealth-maximizing decisions, the typical response is that the system is still better than the alternatives. There may well have been a time when such thinking was valid, but technology and evolving societal norms have changed the playing field. A *wikiocracy* would allow eager and engaged individuals to contribute in significant ways, big and small, without having to become politicians.

Indeed, thinking back once more to my high school days, I was not popular enough to become an elected member of our student council. However, in my later years, I developed a keen interest in political science, probably because of its structures and rules. As a result, I was given the task to review and rewrite the student council's constitution in my final year – not as a politician, or even a formal 'public servant', but merely as a willing and skilled citizen. Sound familiar?

A subtle distinction must be emphasized here: In the system I propose, one person's *vote* will still be worth the same as another's. However, in developing the policies, those who are directly impacted by a decision or who have special expertise will have a greater impact on determining the best ways forward. As well, anyone who chooses to be active and informed on a matter will have greater access to the process. Wikipedia does not designate who are the best people to write its informative entries. But it does recognize that a few people will be much better than most, and it attempts to create a self-regulating forum where those few will be the ultimate authors. Those are the same principles that I envision for a wikiocracy.

A wikiocracy creates the potential for any interested citizen to be better informed and to fully participate at any level of the decision-making process. By meeting those precise requirements for better decisions, we increase the true value of each participant's vote and the ultimate value to society of the outcomes. Such a system offers many of the same benefits of consensus decision-making, but on a much larger scale. Just as importantly, it would eliminate much of the bias and short-term thinking of our current system, and open up our world to a truer form of democracy. Ultimately, it is the quality of the policy-makers, and not wealth or population numbers, that will deliver power to the people in the most meaningful way.

The history of civilization has seen many different styles of social decision-making, from total consensus to dictatorship. The essential message of the disillusioned citizens who founded the Occupy Movement seems to be that when a democracy (rule by the people) is really a plutocracy (rule by wealth), then it is reduced to hypocrisy and no longer legitimate. It is my own hope that some day the prevalent system will be a style of emergent meritocracy (decisions by ability), and that future technology will make it possible for the appropriate individuals – those with the interest and expertise in a particular situation – to help us achieve the best decisions imaginable.

> *In this possibly terminal phase of human existence,*
> *democracy and freedom are more than just ideals to be*
> *valued - they may be essential to survival.*
> *– Noam Chomsky, linguist & philosopher*

Chapter Ten

Our Value Personae

*Black Friday took a grim turn when a New York Wal-Mart
employee died after bargain hunters broke down the doors
to the store, pushing him to the ground. [...] A 28-year-old
pregnant woman was also taken in for observation and three
other shoppers suffered minor injuries during the incident,
police said. [...] Items on sale at the Wal-Mart store
included a $798 Samsung 50-inch Plasma HDTV, a Bissel
Compact Upright Vacuum for $28, a Samsung 10.2
megapixel digital camera for $69 and DVDs such as "The
Incredible Hulk" for $9. – Fox News, Nov. 28, 2008*

WHEN I MOVED FROM the metropolis of Toronto to the rural hills of Caledon, it was not for environmental or financial reasons. I just needed a change, a different pace of life. The new house had great views, overlooking a valley of forests and hills. It also had great winds, which howled from all angles. Within the first few months of moving in, the screen door simply left. I named the place "Aanimad", a native Ojibwe word meaning *"the wind blows wildly here"*.

This was in 2004 when wind-generated power was very topical, especially in Ontario. At the time I knew nothing about renewable energy, nor was I an active environmentalist, but I was curious to learn more. So I took a weekend workshop, and erected a small 1kW wind turbine on the property atop a 50-foot tower. The system supplies electrical power to the house through a battery bank, using a sophisticated inverter to charge the batteries and convert DC power to AC. Not surprisingly, friends, visitors, and neighbours had lots of questions about the project. One question in particular seemed to always come up: "How long before the system pays for itself?"

Truth be told, the savings from small wind systems like mine might never cover their cost so I didn't consider the payback period to be a very important point. For me, the questions were: Could I afford the system without borrowing money? Would I learn lots of new things? Would I be doing the right thing for the environment? I knew that if the answers were yes, the costs would soon be forgotten and the benefits would remain. But for many people, the payback is the only point. If the system won't save more money than it costs, why bother installing it?

It is curious to think how often we worry about wasting money without giving all that much thought to wasting power and planetary resources. Why don't the latter considerations have higher priority on our value scales? This chapter explores the phenomenon of our conflicting value systems and how we might shift to what's better for our future.

Our Seemingly Hypocritical Values

My father is a vigorous supporter of the rights of workers and mistreated employees. He is often a champion of the underdog and has a strong sense of justice. Few things rile him more than the outrageous financial remuneration of those at the very top of the corporate pyramid. He vehemently protests the multi-million dollar salaries, bonuses, pension plans, and severance packages offered to the CEOs of big corporations, and regularly shares anecdotes detailing the most recent example of these egregious payouts. And yet he is equally passionate about playing the stock market, and has substantial investments in a wide variety of equity portfolios, including corporations with the very same compensation plans he finds so objectionable.

Like most of us, my father regularly works against his own values. He becomes infuriated by what he sees as unconscionable behaviour by the senior executives, but at the same time he supports that kind of wealth-seeking thinking with his investment dollars. As an investor he selects stocks for their profitability, but as a citizen he rebels against profligate greed. He would say that it is simply a question of proportion. I think there is a deeper message.

> *The awkward truth is that most of us are of two minds:*
> *As consumers and investors we want the great deals.*
> *As citizens we don't like many of the social consequences*
> *that flow from them. – Robert B. Reich, Supercapitalism*

I, too, am guilty of not always respecting my own values. Living in the rural countryside, I now spend a lot of time tending the household vegetable garden, learning about honey and maple syrup production, and generally living a life that is closer to the land. I contribute time to a local environmental awareness group, and regularly attend gatherings surrounded by people who are hyper-aware of what they are eating, where their clothes are made, and the carbon footprint of their transport. I do my best to emulate their admirable behaviours, but I continually run into personal dilemmas, especially at the grocery store. I try to buy locally-grown food, but not everything can be sourced from nearby. When it comes to the planet-friendly stuff like organic produce and fair-trade foods, I have to be prepared to pay a lot more. As a concerned citizen I want to do the right thing, but as a consumer I am sometimes unwilling to pay the higher prices or give up imported items. It's like I'm of two completely different mindsets, each with different values, and I feel like a hypocrite when I compromise one set for another.

In his book Supercapitalism (2007), Robert B. Reich helps to explain such conflicts. He describes three different value systems which co-exist within each one of us and can be expressed at any moment. These *value personae*, as I like to call them, are: "Citizen", "Investor", and "Consumer". This is a very powerful concept. Think about it: As a *citizen*, chances are you are disturbed by human rights abuses, toxic pollution, job insecurity, the growing gap between rich and poor, rainforest clear-cutting, and all of those pressing concerns of humanity. On the other hand, it is also likely that you are an *investor*, either directly through stocks and mutual funds, or indirectly through a pension fund. As such, you want a high return on your investments. Furthermore, as a *consumer*, you almost certainly appreciate a bargain when you find one, and have at some point taken advantage of big-box retail pricing and product advances in mobile phones, cars, computers, appliances, and pharmaceuticals – often at ever decreasing prices.

> As *citizens*, we value social responsibility and a healthy environment; as *consumers*, we want lower prices and more selection; as *investors*, we want to profit from a continuously growing economy.

It is easy to identify the conflicts between the three value personae. Here are some examples:

Investor vs. Consumer: We want our pension holdings and financial stocks to get good returns, but we want low prices and no banking fees.

Consumer vs. Citizen: We want our magazines, books, and printed reports, but we hate to see our forests razed to generate pulp and paper.

Investor vs. Citizen: We want our pharmaceutical stocks to go up, but we don't want rising drug prices for seniors, the poor, or the developing world.

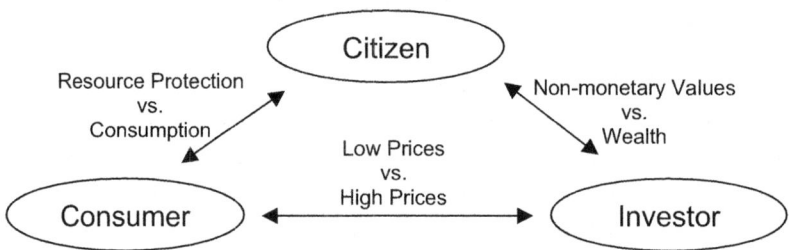

Values in Conflict – So What?

Reich talks about how the values of the *consumer* and *investor* in all of us are in direct opposition to our *citizen* values. Of equal significance, in my view, is the fact that the first two use predominantly number-based value systems, while the third relies on human scales. As we've already seen, these systems are incompatible. However, such value conflicts are so ubiquitous that we have become quite used to resolving them internally. By adopting biases and prioritizations within our overall value system, we can perform everyday tasks like food shopping without agonizing too much in the produce aisle. While we may have some awareness of the values behind our choices, it is not uncommon to completely ignore the tenets of one set of values when we're wearing the hat of another, even though the results might be contrary to our platforms. If a cashier accidentally gives us an extra dollar with our change, we may follow our *consumer/investor* values and keep it, or follow the *citizen* value of returning it. Even many hard-core environmentalists still fly to vacation destinations.

Part of what keeps our value systems in balance is that when monetary values get out of hand, we have a deeper set of human values to draw from. These fundamental human values, which are derived from physiological needs and are perhaps innate, can override conflicting ones, at least within an individual. If the choices suggested by an incompatible value begin to threaten our immediate well-being, our natural instinct for survival can kick in and correct them. Even the compulsive gambler eventually decides to eat. This is one of the reasons why we have been able to deal with these value conflicts for so long.

Consider the following bit of humourous dialogue, loosely attributed to playwright George Bernard Shaw:

A: How do you do? Would you have sex with me for a million dollars?

B: Gracious! That is a very strange request, but yes, I believe I would.

A: How about twenty bucks for a quick one right now?

B: Certainly not! What kind of person do you think I am?

A: We've already established that. Now we're just negotiating the price.

What's amusing is how person B gets tripped up between their *investor* and *citizen* value systems. We ponder at what specific number the value system switches, even within ourselves!

Citizen values are not superior to *consumer* or *investor* values – they are simply different. In the context of this book, what most distinguishes the *citizen* mindset from that of the *consumer* and *investor* is the fundamental realization that *value* and *money* do not mean the same thing. All three value personae are essential to our individual survival: The *consumer* looks after our immediate needs; the *investor* ensures our longer-term survival; and the *citizen* moderates so that neither of the first two pursuits impinges on our collective survival. Even the conflicts between them serve an important purpose, since these value interactions are in fact polar systems. As we have seen, polarities – with their feedback loops and counterbalances – are a necessary characteristic of any sustainable system.

> Our internal *consumer* addresses immediate needs; our *investor* plans for future needs; our *citizen* provides the impulse for collaboration, empathy, moderation, and justice.

We humans seem to have acquired the basic skills required to balance the conflicting desires of our internal *consumer*, *investor*, and *citizen* values. Our innate sense of fairness, equality, and abhorrence of ex-cessive greed comes from one value system; the attraction to low-cost goods, investment opportunities, and playing the stock market comes from the others. Clearly, different individuals adopt these values in different proportions. This is part of what distinguishes the social activist from the commodities trader. Individual bias is okay – a certain amount of specialization leads to efficiency and diversity, both of which are useful.

So why should we care about incompatible value systems? Our society has increasingly relied on monetary economies for thousands of years. Progress continues and humanity flourishes. Aren't these conflicts relatively innocuous? If we can deal with them as they arise, what's the problem?

There are two problems. The first is that the societal background has changed, with a strong bias for numbers. I contend that the domi-nance of number-based value systems is affecting our individual system of checks and balances, rendering them less effective. Monetary value scales tend to outrank other scales for reasons not justified by their actual importance to our needs and motivations. There are plenty of instances in which the quest for money and wealth have driven individuals to perform inhumane and self-destructive acts, and one need

186

look no further than our prisons, casinos, and boardrooms for abundant examples. On a less extreme note, diverse indicators such as rampant consumerism, apathetic waste management, and soaring personal debt suggest that the ability of our human values to override number-based values may well be in decline.

The second and more serious problem is that major societal decisions are very rarely made by single individuals; they're made by groups of people acting collectively – either consciously (e.g. governments) or unconsciously (e.g. trends). These are the decisions that have a huge impact on our world, and like any other dynamic balancing act, our social system only works when all three value personae are equally represented at the decision-making table. When they are not, we run into very large-scale, widespread challenges, and the consequences are potentially devastating.

> *Consumers are different than citizens. Consumers do not have obligations, responsibilities, and duties to their fellow human beings. And as long as you are using that word "consumer" in the public discussion, you will be degrading the quality of the discussion...*
> *– James Howard Kunstler, American author*

Value Personae at the Societal Level

Society has three entities that each represent one of the value personae on a collective level. The "consumer" value set is represented by *the marketplace*. It is the marketplace that demands low prices and more consumer goods in order to meet immediate individual needs. The "investor" value set is represented by *business corporations*. As a whole, these corporations are singularly focused on growing the economy, thereby increasing societal wealth to meet future needs. The "citizen" value set is theoretically represented by *government*, and this is where the problem arises. Most governments today are not focused on protecting citizen values above the interests of the marketplace and the corporations; too often they mistakenly view those values as one and the same. Moreover, corporations and the marketplace each embody a single value system: that of numbers. They have no internal facility to override excesses with human values.

187

> Free markets look after *consumers* and *investors*, but their number-based value system renders them incapable of caring for the values of *citizens*.

For this reason, we need an equally powerful entity to moderate market actions so that they don't impinge on our survival. Governments are in the best position to assume this role. Firstly, they are intended to represent every single member of their population, regardless of income level. Secondly, they regulate their own income through taxation, so they need not wholly rely on the consumer or investor value systems to survive.

> The single most important role of governments is to represent *citizen* values, not the monetary-based *consumer* and *investor* values.

Unfortunately, this is where our modern form of civilization has fallen out of balance. Instead of exclusively representing the values of the *citizens*, our governments have taken on the completely false mandate of perpetually growing the economy, to the benefit of the *investor* value set. (It doesn't help that surplus personal wealth is a near prerequisite to get yourself elected. For example, as of 2012, the majority of U.S. Congress and Senate members were millionaires.) The representation of *citizen* values, such as social justice, culture, morality, and environmental stewardship is now centred in non-profit organizations, religious congregations, and ever-shrinking remnants of the public sector. These groups, with their inability to compete on a monetary playing field, are fighting a losing battle. As a result, the conflicts between our *citizen* values and the two number-based systems are no longer managed, and the system is rapidly losing stability.

The care of human life and happiness, and not their
destruction, is the first and only object of good government.
– Thomas Jefferson, American president (1743-1826)

The monetary value system of corporations has not changed significantly in over a century. And yet, the prominence of commercialism, the social effects of globalization, the decline of the public sector and its regulatory influence, and the devastation of the planet's environment have all experienced a dramatic acceleration in the last few decades. Given that material wealth has been a driving force in our civilization for centuries, why is this *value crisis* happening now?

Robert B. Reich offers compelling historical reasons for the current state of affairs. He posits that the process began with a technological explosion, fuelled partly by massive defence contractor budgets during the Cold War. The resulting advances in transportation (container shipping, jet aircraft), electronics (integrated circuits, personal computers), telecommunications (fibre optics, satellites), and of course the internet itself, have all come together to completely rewrite the way industry works. This has destabilized pre-existing balances between business, labour, and government, and even between nations.

Essentially what happened is that the state of competition changed. Predictability and market oligopolies (a stable combination of democracy and capitalism, which Reich calls "democratic capitalism") gave way to unprecedented innovation, market access, consumer choice, and overnight successes of start-ups. With communication and shipping advances came the ability for labour to be easily tapped anywhere in the world. The arrival of the digital age meant that even the smallest manufacturer could use computer-controlled machinery to produce products and parts of comparable quality to the large industry players. With access to equivalent software and other technologies, market newcomers could successfully compete with established airlines, banks, pharmaceutical firms, and phone companies. Anyone with a computer could now create an internet presence – sometimes one that was practically indistinguishable from that of the largest corporations. Suddenly, every commercial field was wide open. Consumers, manufacturers, and investors were now shopping the world instead of their community.

In order to remain competitive, the existing major industry leaders pushed for deregulation in their sectors. This freed them up to compete with the new threats to their market share, but it also opened up the floodgates to more entrants. It used to be that society feared the huge corporations because of the potential for collusion, monopolies, and unfairly high prices. While that is still a valid concern, we now see a new phenomenon: The level of competition can be such that the biggest players, like Wal-Mart, continue to drive prices and costs *down*, not up, even though they have market dominance, thereby depressing salaries and putting rivals out of business. To compound the situation, online access to financial data and share trading has led to vast numbers of smaller investors with easy movement of any capital that isn't generating wealth fast enough. Corporations are increasingly competing not just for consumers but also for investors.

Reich believes that the shift from "democratic capitalism" to what he calls "supercapitalism" has resulted in a global level of competition that gives corporations no choice but to pursue a mandate of profit regardless of the external costs. Political lobbying and purchased government influence are now critical to their survival. Any attempt to act to the contrary, even in the interests of public good, will be punished immediately by both consumers and investors.

This means that the value crises we face as the *citizen* are a direct result of our actions as *consumer* and *investor*. The people who are consuming and investing are often precisely the same people who are outraged by widening income gaps, the degradation of social values, and the destruction of the environment. Corporations, on the other hand, operate by one value system only, and are caught in the middle. They bear the brunt of the blame, when, in reality, the value clash is our own.

> It is *our actions* as consumers and investors that sustain the cut-throat level of competition between corporations. The relentless drive for lower costs and higher profits comes from us, not from them.

It is critical that we recognize our role in the motivation and sustenance of business corporations. It is counterproductive and hypocritical for society to blame environmental degradation and oil spills on multinational oil companies, when those corporations are simply trying to keep up with the high demand that we create, and meet the profit targets that we expect of them. Once we adopt the pursuit of wealth as a reasonable primary objective, we are also adopting a linear, number-based value system, which ignores *externalities* (costs borne by others) and does not recognize the concept of sufficiency.

Separation of Public and Private Sectors

Given their inherent conflicts, it is necessary for all three value personae to be adequately and separately represented at the highest levels of our society. By its very nature, the world of commerce will take care of the number-based monetary values. It is therefore up to governments to represent our citizen values. Not only should their policies and actions reflect unquantifiable human values, I maintain that they should do so exclusively. This is not to say that governments should be fiscally irresponsible, only that their values must be non-numeric.

A key mandate of any government is to mitigate the overwhelming power of big business by representing the human value systems of its people. Governments that rely on corporations to stay in power cannot perform their responsibilities effectively. Unfortunately, our society continues to move further and further away from an adequate balance of value systems because we allow monetary wealth to influence our governments. This may have been historically tolerable when the wealthy players ruling the game were still human, but now we have far more powerful entities at work with less diverse values: corporations. Despite their claims to legal personhood, corporations are not citizens. They have no rights to vote and should not unduly influence the decision-making capacity of the public sector. Corporations are already part of another kind of 'democracy', the one in which we vote with our dollars. The only forum where corporations should hold sway is the marketplace, not the legislature or political backroom.

> Corporations are *not* citizens and should have no participative role in government. The power of industry lobbies should never exceed the power of our regulatory government agencies.

191

Given that deregulation leads to runaway competition and business excesses, I submit that we should strive for increased regulation of industry by government. True, consumers may pay more for certain goods, but the payoff in stability and responsible corporate behaviour is worth the price. There are those who fanatically defend deregulation and privatization, believing that a free market will regulate itself and do a much better job of things. However, such advocates do not appreciate the narrow, inflexible principles and short-sightedness of quantitative value systems. At best, free markets will look after *consumers* and *investors*, but they are incapable of prioritizing the needs of *citizens*. The human-based values of *citizens* must not only be recognized, they must come first for a while until a more sustainable balance is achieved.

This might seem contrary to economist Adam Smith's *Theory of the Invisible Hand*, which suggests that in a pure *laissez-faire* economic system a capitalist marketplace will inherently produce outcomes that are good for society: If corporations act against the greater good, the marketplace will punish them. The problem with this theory is how you define what is good for society. Each value set will have its own answer, which complicates and even impairs the feedback mechanisms of the *Invisible Hand*. In today's world of massive corporate players, the challenge becomes the time it takes for the marketplace to respond, and whether we can live with the resulting scope of that response.

As I was writing an early draft of this book, the United States government was borrowing more than $700 billion to cover the debts of its financial industry, caused by mismanagement, irresponsible risk-taking, practices bordering on fraud, and staggering payouts to individual players. If the market were truly permitted to regulate itself, then such profligate entities would be eradicated by the market itself. Furthermore, self-regulation would determine that tragically defective economies *should* collapse. Major car makers were poised to fail, potentially prompting a radical re-evaluation of automotive design and our policies on transport and oil consumption. In that respect, yes, the theory holds and the market should have been allowed to manage itself.

Alas, it was not – the judgements of the marketplace were ignored. Instead, the corporations were bailed out, and every attempt was made to restore the grossly flawed status quo. This was because by the time the government recognized their mandate to protect the citizens it was too late to do anything else. System-mandated corporate failure is not an option when the stakes are so high that human values like trust, justice, and national livelihood are threatened. Could there ever be a better example of how free-rein, unregulated capitalism can cripple a society that, by necessity, must also respect non-monetary values? The only way to avoid such dilemmas is to regulate up front.

As radical and unfamiliar as it may seem, I propose that our governments should essentially be working as a balancing counter-weight to economic forces. If they don't, who will? If the planet's resources are not better managed and non-monetary values are not represented by a powerful force equal to that of the corporations and the marketplace, then those resources and values will eventually be abused by us and disappear. Economists are already familiar with this threat, calling it the *Tragedy of the Commons*.

Neither corporations nor the marketplace can ever be expected to safeguard our moral values. It is a mistake to consider them as being composed of individuals able to express all three value personae. Those institutions respectively represent the *investor* persona and *consumer* persona only, and their group value systems are both monetary. Period. By the same token, it is not the responsibility of government to safeguard jobs or keep industries alive. The marketplace already has mechanisms to resolve changes caused by the ebb and flow of the economy. Attempts by the public sector to rescue the economy simply short-circuit the market forces already in place, and undermine the government's real mandate: to represent the human-based value system of the *citizens*, to institute justice, to enforce social values, and to create legislation for the greater good.

The Inevitable Pain of Value Transitions

The fact that there are three distinct value systems at play here is fundamental to explaining why we are unable to make progress on the things that need to be done to resolve our value crisis. Any action taken to improve society's well-being on one scale will naturally take it down on another. Strategies for decreasing our society's unsustainable addiction to consumerism will have immediate and unpleasant effects on our employment rates and return on investments. Take for example our pulp and paper mill industry. Most people would agree that we cut down far too many trees and that deforestation is devastating our environment. In fact, paper was one of the first things in the world to be widely recycled in an attempt to reduce the number of forests converted into pulp for packaging and newspapers. Typically, it was our governments that instigated these recycling programs in response to our demands as citizens. Yet these self-same governments continue to bail out financially strapped pulp and paper mills, and frantically seek new markets for their products. Why? Wasn't that the point – to reduce the demand for paper? Should we not be celebrating whenever a mill closes its doors?

I don't mean to downplay the social and financial consequences of allowing industries to fold, but I believe we fail to grasp the alternative. A continuance of the status quo is a mathematical impossibility and profound changes are inevitable. We can either manage those changes now or have the rug pulled out from under our unsustainable systems in the future. The former may be painful, but the latter will be devastating. This is analogous to Canada's east coast fishery, whose growth was maintained in order to keep the economy afloat despite dire warnings from biologists. The result, of course, was a catastrophic depletion of fish stocks and total industry collapse.

Perhaps the most significant obstacle to strengthening the influence of human values is that such changes will adversely affect our monetary status quo. This is inevitable, but to consider it an overall negative is to miss the point entirely. When a critical problem is identified within one value system, such as citizens decrying the depletion or toxicity of our fresh water supply, we must not allow the discussion to be taken out of that value system or debate actions solely on their economic merits. Money cannot be allowed to trump survival.

It is precisely our pursuit of never-ending economic growth that is threatening our planetary resources in the first place. The public sector should not be using private sector value systems to drive policy. I don't propose that governments participate in devastating the lives of industry workers – I suggest that they provide the transitional safety nets and implement better solutions for all their citizens.

One of the most respected and controversial economists of recent history was Milton Friedman, a Nobel laureate who was renowned for his opposition to taxes and any kind of government interference in the economy. I completely agree with his assertion that government regulation is often bad for business. However, I also think that this in itself is a good thing. While he assumed that unfettered business and never-ending economic expansion is ultimately good for humanity, such a strategy is totally unsustainable. Indeed, many forward-thinking businesses actually support increased regulation, so that they can act in a responsible manner without losing market share to those that don't. If doing the right thing costs money, it has to apply to everyone.

Separating government from industry and balancing the powers of the two is far from easy, but progress is being made. There's a growing trend around the world to limit or remove the ability of corporations to make donations to political parties and politicians (with the notable exception of the United States, which is disturbingly going in the other direction). Such initiatives should be supported and expanded until the practice is eliminated once and for all. The next step is to increasingly regulate and limit the power of corporate lobbyists. All of these monetary influences and obligations belong to a different value system, and serve to at best dilute – and at worst corrupt – the relevant value systems of our governments.

> *The question is never whether the state regulates*
> *corporations – it always does – but how, and in whose*
> *interests, it does so. Beguiled by the "natural entity"*
> *conception of corporations, the notion that they are*
> *independent persons, we tend to forget that they are entirely*
> *dependent upon the state for their creation and*
> *empowerment. – Joel Bakan, The Corporation*

In Summary

We began this chapter by asking why we care more about saving money than about saving our environment or preserving the planet for future generations. The truth is that we care about all three things. Inside each one of us are three distinct value systems: the citizen, the consumer, and the investor, which are in constant conflict and can be expressed at any time. However, our citizen persona, which represents our human values, is in serious danger of being overwhelmed. This is partly because the consumer and investor personae are based on number-based value systems, which have no concept of "enough". It is also because major corporations have usurped the public agenda with their message of unfettered economic growth.

More than half of the world's 100 largest economic entities are corporations, not nations. This phenomenal ascendance, which Reich calls supercapitalism, is an important context for the crisis we are now experiencing. However, at a deeper level, I suggest that its root cause is systemic, going back much further than the previous century. Our value crisis is the inevitable consequence of the most basic differences between the way numeric and non-numeric value systems work. The linearity of numbers mean that we can only increase value in one direction, and also that success is determined by constant growth, regardless of its deleterious effects. Humanity's survival, on the other hand, depends upon a delicate interplay of value structures, which are constantly shifting and responding to the environment and the people around us.

If we continue to defer to the entities with the most money, then value systems which measure success by happiness, equity, and sustainability will be permanently side-lined. This is not just a question of our quality of life in the future; it is a question of our very survival as a species. Monetary concerns impose their math on our value systems to an incredible degree, but money does not respect our needs as a species, nor our innate human values. Math is not concerned with our self-preservation.

Recall that the *citizen* value persona is the one that ensures the needs of others are respected. This refers not only to the needs of our fellow planetary inhabitants, but also to the needs of the generations that will follow us. The undeniable truth is that we are very heavily borrowing from the resources, financial stability, and living conditions of future generations just to keep the numbers of the current *investor* and *consumer* systems going. We are literally stealing from the survival of our grandchildren in order to line our own pockets.

The essential message of this chapter, and indeed of this book, is not a call to eradicate big business in order to let nature prosper. Rather, the management of this value crisis begins with an awareness that our human values are being ignored at the highest levels of society, and that we have only ourselves to blame. The only way to rebalance this deficit is to demand that governments abandon their obsession with economic growth and concern themselves solely with championing the non-quantitative values of their citizens.

Any extrication from this value crisis is going to involve pain, hardship, and the reversal of widespread assumptions of entitlement, but if civilization is to continue, we must make changes to our way of life. By all accounts, these choices will be financially difficult and impossible to justify in terms of economics. Again, *money* and *value* are not the same thing.

> Actions taken to improve humanity's prospects
> for survival will have negative *economic*
> consequences. The value of such actions will
> need to be measured on *other* scales.

Returning to the microcosm world of my wind turbine, it was indeed other scales that I needed to measure it by. The best available data suggested it would never pay for itself. Instead, I learned plenty about renewable energy and developed a phenomenal awareness of power consumption in my home. I also gained an enviable independence from the grid during power outages. But it turned out that my consumer and investor needs got met, after all. Soon after installing the wind turbine, I developed software to monitor its output. Selling this software to other renewable energy system owners ultimately provided a totally unplanned-for source of income – more than making up for the initial investment. I'm not suggesting that putting our citizen's needs first will always satisfy the consumer and investor as well, but they need not be mutually exclusive.

We live in a world where success and survivability are largely mea-sured in dollars and cents. This is a simple fact of life in our modern civilization, but it doesn't have to be our future. The tide can change;

we can choose different values. Since all three value personae reside in each of us, so too does the power to resolve the crisis we're in.

> *The hope of free man in a frightened world is the values*
> *which man puts ahead of inventions when his back is to the*
> *wall. These values are beauty, truth, goodness and having a*
> *faith, all of which are bombproof.*
> *– Ralph W. Sockman, pastor (1889–1970)*

Conclusion

So What's Next?

A crisis is a terrible thing to waste.
– Paul Romer, economist

M OST OF THIS BOOK is devoted to discussing numbers and number-based values. Since I refer to our present predicament as a value *crisis*, it is perhaps useful to close with a look at the idea of "crisis" itself. While the term is commonly applied to a catastrophic system failure, it also describes a situation that will inevitably lead to such a failure. I define it by our awareness: We are *in* a crisis when we become *aware* of that catastrophic system failure – either by its future inevitability or by its effects raining down upon us.

An old friend once told me that I was at my best when there was a crisis afoot. Perhaps it's not surprising then that my two current volunteer pursuits deal heavily with crisis, though in very different ways. As a member of a Red Cross Disaster Management Team, I am tasked with responding to all kinds of crises, from residential house fires to large-scale regional disasters. As the facilitator of a local Transition Town group, I work with a small collective devoted to increasing community resilience and lowering dependence on fossil fuels, in anticipation of a looming energy crisis. Crisis, unfolding or anticipated, is the one thing these groups have in common, and the lessons from my time with each provide an interesting framework for the conclusion to this book.

But first, a brief review is in order...

The Value Crisis in a Nutshell

We live in a world in which numbers and number-based values have become both our lens and our filter. Without us necessarily being conscious of it, they influence how we make decisions, define success, and measure progress. Human values, which have served us well through millennia of evolution, are taking a back seat. It is this crisis – a value crisis – that has created a long list of threats to our survival, including environmental degradation, economic collapse, shrinking supplies of fossil fuels, ever-widening wealth disparity, climate change, and a diminished sense of well-being (even when it looks like we have everything).

The unidirectional linearity of number-based value systems demands constant growth in order to achieve constant value increases. But as we know, a future based on limitless mathematics is impossible on a planet with limited assets. Our frantic attempts to maintain the status quo have resulted in our present wealth existing as debt – a debt that has already surpassed the capacity of our finite resources to ever settle. We now have singularly profit-focused corporations holding incredible power over our resources and our governments. Indeed, our governments have largely abdicated their mandate to represent human values, focusing instead on how to maintain a constantly growing economy. Our own value conflicts between our inner consumer, investor, and citizen have collectively left us incapable of mounting a coordinated and unified response. Unfortunately for us, a system collapse of one form or another is inevitable.

Portrait of a Crisis

How will this system collapse manifest itself? What does the climax of a global value crisis look like? Disturbing hints are showing up with increasing frequency. Perhaps it will begin with a massive spike in oil prices, or a European country's economic collapse, or a rebellion of the unemployed, or another bout of hyperinflation, or a misjudged plummet over a fiscal cliff. Or maybe it will be triggered by a series of cataclysmic climate events. It might be sudden or it might take months for the full effects to be felt by all.

The fact that we appear to have dodged this bullet a few times, like with the financial meltdown of 2008, does not in any way lower the probability that a full collapse will eventually happen. Indeed, we pull ourselves out of these close calls by borrowing even more heavily from our future. 'Recovery' policies like *quantitative easing*, a euphemistic term for when the financial sector simply creates more and more money with nothing to back it up, show that we are like a family addicted to debt, but on a global level. The bill will eventually arrive – even the numbers say it has to.

Might it be possible to change our ways before the axe falls, thus sidestepping the global catastrophe? Probably not. To begin with, a tranquil change of society's predominant value system is not likely to come from the top, because not surprisingly there is insufficient incentive for the wealthiest corporations and citizens to make such a radical change. There is also the 'Catch-22' that you won't change your value system until you see a clear benefit of doing so, and such benefits are only visible if you first change your value system. A shift will only occur when the current system is no longer working for people. So, if a societal reassertion of non-numeric human values is ever going to take place, I can think of two ways in which it could happen.

In the first scenario, a substantial minority of people gradually start to abandon the goal of financial prosperity, get out of debt, shift their personal value systems, and pursue fewer consumption-oriented objectives. Finding themselves happier with life, they begin to influence others, until a movement occurs that causes a complete paradigm shift in our society. While this might be something to strive for, it is frankly not very probable. The forces opposing it are just too strong.

In the second (and more likely) scenario, the change is externally imposed when one or more of the crisis predictions comes true and our global financial economy collapses like a house of cards. The current value system would no longer be working for anybody, and there would be a necessity for everyone to seriously revisit what is important to them and their communities.

Crisis as Opportunity

There's a popular catch phrase, especially amongst U.S. presidents and twenty-first century business consultants, that the Chinese characters for "crisis" (*wēijī*) are made up of their characters for "danger" and "opportunity". This is a marvellous and uplifting call to action when things are at their bleakest. Unfortunately, this particular example of prescient etymological wisdom is totally false. The *wēi* character does indeed mean "danger", but the *jī* character is more accurately translated as "crucial point or critical juncture". In other words, the Chinese have exactly the same definition for "crisis" that we do: a crucial time of great danger.

I suspect that this western linguistic myth came from anecdotal evidence combined with a New Age desire to sell business thinkers on seeing numerical opportunities in any sort of crisis. When a situation arises that presents significant danger to humans and human values, it is very hard to see this as a good thing. But shift your perspective to a number-based value system, and suddenly the opportunities become clear. Throughout the ages, for example, wars have often pulled the victorious nations (and sometimes even the defeated ones) out of economic slumps. This tradition of profit-from-conflict continues through the defence contracts of the Cold War, the exponential growth of private security forces since 9/11, and reconstruction projects in post-war Iraq.

Some people, such as author Naomi Klein in <u>The Shock Doctrine,</u> have even suggested that modern corporations manufacture crises in order to disrupt the status quo, suppress opposition to new policies, and ultimately take advantage of the chaos to increase profits. While this might seem far-fetched, I certainly support the idea that number-based value systems can usually find positive opportunities in situations that seem entirely negative for human values. More than one billionaire has been created through the investor's creed: "Buy Fear, Sell Greed."

But what if the shoe is on the other foot? What if it is the number-based value system that collapses – the system that defines monetary value, demands economic growth, drives our insatiable appetite for resources, etc. Could this be an opportunity for human values? I believe so. In fact, I'll go one step further and say that a worldwide economic collapse could actually be the best thing that could happen to us now. Allow me to explain...

A catastrophe is more than a jarring wake-up call: It has the dual effects of dismantling existing systems while also inspiring instinctive human behaviours. For most of us in the West, our exposure to 'crisis' is relatively minor, but we can still discern some predictable outcomes.

My work as a Red Cross volunteer sometimes puts me in the midst of those affected by tragic property loss or natural disasters such as floods, hurricanes, and ice storms. Observing human behaviour in such situations can give one a unique perspective on how we cope with crisis and system failures. Perhaps you have experienced a similar crisis in the form of a unexpected death in the family, a neighbourhood house fire, a serious traffic accident, an extended power outage, or a sudden loss of employment. Chances are that you came together with other people in uncommon ways – having powerful (even positive) interactions that you would not otherwise have had. A crisis throws assumptions and excuses out the window; there is a pause and a re-evaluation of what is truly important.

At the outbreak of the Second World War, entire production lines were changed overnight, food gardens were started, people consumed less, and whole communities reorganized around new priorities. We know this can be done. Of course, that doesn't alter the fact that a catastrophe is accompanied by extreme difficulty and terrible hardship. A total economic collapse would very likely result in widespread anarchy, desperation, violence, food shortages, and even epidemics, as our reliance on financial wealth suddenly became meaningless. Goods would no longer be made or moved, and essential services would no longer be offered. The energy consumption that we now take for granted would simply not be a possibility. This would indeed be a disaster of unprecedented scope for humanity.

It would be callous and insulting to suggest that such a crisis is really just an opportunity. It is not a scenario that anyone would ever wish to experience. Yet the numbers clearly tell us that the collapse is inevitable. The good news is that a global crisis need not be a personal crisis. If this event is indeed probable within the next decade or two, what can we do about it? Assuming that it is too late or unrealistic to avert such a thing, the best way to soften the blow of any disaster, be it personal or global, is to prepare for it.

For some, this already means stockpiling food caches and weapons to protect what's 'theirs' – a vision that's disheartening and frightening, to say the least. They are preparing for an economic shift, but not the value shift that we so desperately need. I offer a different perspective.

The Best in a Worst Case Scenario

Let's consider a numeric-value 'worst case' scenario: a full-on world-wide economic depression. Technically, a depression is simply a long-term downturn in economic activity – the opposite of growth. We often associate the concept with its twin in psychology parlance, but unhappiness and despair are not *inevitable* outcomes. To illustrate this with an extreme example, imagine living in beautiful homes on a tropical island with all of your friends, plenty of food, and lots to do, all at no cost – zero economic activity – the epitome of depressions. Would this really trigger unhappiness and despair? I think not. No, it is only when we handcuff our joy in life to the numerical success of the economy that our misery in an economic depression is assured. Our only hope is to shift our value systems.

The working class will bear the initial brunt of an economic downturn – they always do – but the effects will now be felt all the way up the chain. Would it really be so bad for the number of cars per person to decrease and for the density of some housing to increase (i.e. more people living in multi-unit buildings)? If the same real estate must now support larger extended families, could that not be seen as a good thing? When people start to take greater care in where they spend their dwindling cash reserves, they will begin to choose repair over throw-away and replace. People might share more skills and tools, and spend more time working together with their neighbours. When the market is unable to support the shipment of frivolous or cheap goods from around the globe, the result will be a greater reliance on local goods and greater community self-sufficiency. And what an improvement it would be if the concept of creating wealth using math alone, as is current practice with our financial institutions and exchanges, was no longer considered to be generating value or contributing to communities.

Unemployment will sky-rocket, but only in a technical sense: the monetary compensation for our labour may disappear, but then, money would no longer have the value that it had. Nowadays, unemployment can constitute a personal crisis because so much is at stake. And yet, none of the basic human benefits of employment (providing food, shelter, sense of identity, and social contact; contributing to the greater good; fulfilling one's life purpose; etc.) have monetary activity as a prerequisite. They could easily be achieved in a self-sustaining community – no paycheques required. Under strictly number-based value systems, huge numbers of unemployed would mean huge numbers of homeless people, but such thinking need not apply. The housing capacity does not disappear when an entire population loses their jobs. When money is no longer king, common sense has a chance to prevail. Such challenges no longer have the same effect.

We're told that there is more than enough food production capacity to feed everyone. But it will take human effort to manage it better and waste less. When cheap fossil fuels are no longer readily available, many tasks will take a lot more manpower and ingenuity. Instead of mechanically extracting new resources, we'll have to spend more time recovering what we already have and repairing what we used to throw away. In other words, there will be more than enough 'work' to keep everyone as busy as they would ever want to be. A surplus of available labour can make a great many positive pursuits practical again – things like artistry, personal touches, and approaches that save materials instead of time. This is not a call for a return to the manual labour of the Middle Ages. Instead, it is an opportunity to do all those positive actions that are now considered "a waste of time" – actions that re-introduce the values of quality, workmanship, pride, and durability.

A slowing down of the economy could be our greatest gift to the environment. The entirely unsustainable activities caused by our insatiable appetite for the world's resources will be gradually reduced. Less disposable income worldwide might translate into better management of raw materials and waste. Our demand for energy would decline, industrial expansion would diminish, and the pace of technological advancement for things like consumer electronics might slow to the point where obsolescence is again measured in years instead of months. Advances in medicine and science need not be driven solely by the pursuit of profit and they don't need to stop. Progress can still be impelled by other values!

Easing the Transition

Of course the time to discover such paradigm shifts is now. That is by far the best preparation for our value crisis. There are pockets of people who are not sitting back and waiting for the system collapse to happen. These include environmental activists, intentional communities, the Occupy Movement, and others who are standing up for the values they believe are being lost in the economic shuffle. Their diverse approaches all began with a value system shift – it is not possible to start with anything less.

> *No problem can be solved from the same level of*
> *consciousness that created it. – Albert Einstein*

To paraphrase Albert Einstein, no value crisis can be solved from the same value system that created it.

In 2005, the Town Council of Kinsale, a small village in Ireland, made a pioneering decision to begin preparing their community for the after-effects of climate change and *peak oil.* (Peak oil is that point in time when the maximum rate of crude oil extraction from the planet is reached, after which extraction rates begin to decline.) In doing so, they became the first of what is now a network of over 475 Transition Towns scattered all over the world. Transition Initiatives are not your typical collection of environmental activists. Both their objective and their methodology are somewhat unique.

To begin with, they tend not to stand in opposition to things; instead they work to promote positive things. The importance of this approach cannot be overstated. I was officially introduced the Transition movement a few years ago when I participated in a workshop near my home community. At first, some of the visions expressed seemed pretty far-fetched and utopian. The status quo of a global society devoted to (and dependent on) economic growth, and fuelled by oil and resource extraction, seemed too powerful a force to alter. Suddenly, it struck me that this transition work was not about trying to turn that massive ship around. It was about planning new headings and the effective use of the lifeboats when the ship goes down. Transition Initiatives don't attempt to change society in order to *prevent* these seminal events. Instead the members focus on readying their community for surviving and thriving beyond the economic and social paradigm shifts that are sure to come. They don't need to go into whether or not we are causing climate change – what's more important to them is that it is most certainly happening and what do we do about that. They are also not the secluded stockpiling survivalists of past decades. They appreciate the potential hardships that lie ahead, but their focus is on the joy that can be had when your lifestyle focuses on community and collaboration. In other words, the actions they encourage can significantly improve our quality of life right now, regardless of external circumstances. There are positive rewards and a net benefit, even if by some miracle no disaster ever came to pass.

Furthermore, while their objective is to determine how to make communities more resilient for life in a post-fossil fuel world, their methodology is all about *value system transition*. Much of their resilience planning revolves around creating local sustainable economies that focus on relationships and quality over growth. In other words, they are working to restore the fundamental human values that lost ground to number-based values in the last century. These are exactly the steps that I propose be taken in response to the value crisis.

As an example, consider the diversity of tangible benefits from the development of local economies. From an economic perspective, local trade sustains the wealth of the community instead of leveraging global disparities for the benefit of a few. From an environmental perspective, there are huge benefits to reducing the transport of goods and having consumers able to see the impacts of production. From a resilience perspective, increasing localized autonomy and self-sufficiency is crucial. However, it is the direct human value perspective where I believe the greatest impact will be felt. When the person selling you a product is the person who made it or grew it, and you both live in the same community, there is a profound value shift. The vendor will likely feel a personal responsibility towards the quality of the product and your decision to buy it. There is pride in the quality of the materials and work or growing methods, and there is real joy in experiencing a meaningful buyer/seller relationship – a human connection. That has genuine value, leading to a different kind of wealth, reflected in the quality of life instead of the standard of living.

Of course, you don't need to join a movement to make a difference. Anyone can adopt a lifestyle of voluntary simplicity and make their own discovery of what genuine wealth means to them. But it's a lot easier and more fun to do it with friends.

The Last Word

The most important effect of rethinking our societal value systems will be a change in how we measure things like success, progress, and happiness, both as individuals and as communities. Our society and our planet are not the same as they were in 1950 or 1975. If we all recognize that, we should also be able to recognize that some behaviours and value decisions that worked for us back then now have a lack of currency.

If we can accept that financial wealth is only a *means* to some higher objective, then we clearly must determine what that higher objective is, and act accordingly. This change must apply to society as a whole, but it also has relevance to every one of us. Knowing your own higher objective gives purpose to your life. Goals measured on number-based values, such as wealth, are problematic and ultimately unsatisfying. It is better to focus on human values: doing what you love; improving health; finding balance; making positive changes in your community; nurturing relationships; helping others; feeding mind, body, and spirit in equal proportions; and valuing quality over quantity.

The value conflicts of society are mostly larger manifestations of our individual value conflicts. Our *consumer* still has to eat, our *investor* will still put aside for the future, but our *citizen* must also be heard and empowered. Resolving our value crisis will not be achieved by rising up against external forces or giant corporations, although we do need to regain control and balance. What is needed is a fundamental recognition of non-numeric values at the individual level, and a return to having human values effectively represented by governments at the group level. The essential message of this work is *not* that number-based value systems are wrong, but that they are unsustainable as the primary foundation of civilization's decision-making, and it is time to question their precedence. Now more than ever, we need a shift in society's *value polarity* towards the pole of human-based values.

I believe that our reliance on the monetary value system has super-seded so many core values that we've put even our instinct for survival as a species at stake. Yet, to condemn money is as nonsensical as to condemn mathematics. Our value crisis is not a battle of right and wrong. It is about making conscious choices that give basic human values the priority they deserve. Numeric and monetary value systems should not hold the dominant position in the human value hierarchy. Correcting that at the societal level may soon be imposed on us by nature or the economy, but I recommend questioning the paradigm at a personal level before that happens. We may just discover that our quality of life rises with a shift of perception. For me, writing this book has inspired many changes to the journey ahead – perhaps it will do so for you too.

The reader's own wisdom begins where that of the author ends. – Marcel Proust, writer (1871-1922)

P.S. The discussion doesn't have to end just because the book does. I welcome your feedback and questions at www.TheValueCrisis.com. Please join in and share your perspectives and ideas with others online.

Also, be sure to check out <u>Our Second Chance</u> – the solution-focused sequel to <u>The Value Crisis</u>. This follow up book, reworked throughout the COVID-19 pandemic, is a must-read for those who wish to understand the challenges in our new world context and translate them into action and progress.

OUR SECOND CHANCE – CHANGING COURSE AND SOLVING THE VALUE CRISIS

published by Captus Press, is available now from https://TheValueCrisis.com

Acknowledgements

Thank you to my dedicated readers and advisors: Elswyth Fryer, Ian Chaprin, Rhonda Sullivan, Kathryn and Peter Turke, Carolyn Burke, Dick Crowther, Derek Demierre, Reed Thomas, Mike Nickerson, Steve Rapaport, Bernadette Hardaker, Elvira Gonnella, Philip Welch, Nancy Early, Nancy Frater, Suzanne Carter, Val Steinmann, Brent Klassen, and Nicola Ross for their most valuable feedback, contributions, and support over the eight years it took to complete this work. Also thanks to fellow writers Aaron Sheedy, Mark Anielski, Harry Posner, and Paul Kennedy for their practical tips and encouragement.

I also want to recognize the patience and professionalism of Sheila Britton, who created several masterful cover designs, and ultimately went beyond my interference and indecision to a superb end result.

Most significantly, this work would be little more than long-winded ramblings without the Herculean efforts of two extremely generous individuals. First, my sincere thanks to Mirjam Urfer, who unwittingly became my first editor. Her uncanny ability to put her finger on the missing, the inappropriate, or the unnecessary covered everything from punctuation and typos, through words and paragraphs, to explanations and ideas. By her guiding my efforts, this book is an order of magnitude better than what I first submitted to her.

Finally, I am hugely indebted to Michele Fisher, my second editor, who took on my cause as one of her own and devoted untold hours to clarifying my message. She gave the work its flow, pruned the proliferation of excess verbiage, reorganized sections, added relevance, rebuilt sentences, and applied her professional eye to the elements of style. She also championed the completion of the work when I had all but given up hopes of it ever being good enough to print. Thank you.

Perhaps against the better judgement of both my editors, when it comes to punctuation, I made a decision to adopt my own combination of rational British and conventional American publishing formats. That choice and all the flaws that remain in this book are mine alone.

Key Ideas Summary

Throughout this book, where significant and original concepts are introduced, I have highlighted them in boxed text. These key ideas are summarized here, with a page reference to where they can be found in context in the chapters.

Numbers are extremely powerful, but without context, they have no meaning in a qualitative human value system.

page 27

Number-based value systems are **limitless**, **linear**, and **consistent**, while innate human value systems have none of those properties.

page 32

Prospect theory can be used to identify three dangers of number-based values: a moving reference point, short-term loss aversion, and a declining sensitivity to affluence.

page 48

Decisions using number-based values are easy to make, easy to defend, and seemingly less susceptible to our innate numerical irrationalities.

page 49

The more we suppress our own value systems, the less familiar we will be with exactly what they are.

page 49

Money has evolved from an *object* you needed for survival, to a *currency* that might buy what you needed for survival, to a *number in a database* that you need to trust for survival.

page 56

Globalization and outsourcing are not just exploitations of economic gaps. They are profit at the expense of other value systems.

page 63

Money and wealth have acquired incredible stature as universal motivators, despite the fact that we have no *innate* need for money at all.

page 72

The monetary value system's definition of success is uniquely unconditional. Wealth confers irrefutable power, easily measured and easily wielded.

page 79

There is a limit to satisfying primary human needs. Once the need has been satisfied, excess quantities do not produce additional benefit.

page 80

Increased wealth will produce an increase in *standard of living*, but once a certain threshold is reached, more money will not make us *happier*.

page 81

Placing a high relative value on time actually increases unemployment and/or demands unsustainable economic expansion, while concentrating wealth in the hands of the few.

page 88

Taxing raw material extraction instead of labour would increase market sustainability, product quality, consumer satisfaction, and employment.

page 90

The investment of money-earning hours to increase your happiness has a peak value, after which additional hours produce the opposite effect.

page 99

More than 99% of the money in our economy is created by banks through loans, representing future value that *does not yet exist.*

page 111

Usury is the acquisition of wealth from others using only mathematics, with no risk, effort, sacrifice, or value-adding contribution. Until fairly recently, it was *always* considered unethical.

page 115

Platonic banking would offer an alternative that returns to the original function of money: a storage for wealth with no fractional reserve, no interest, no investment, and no debt.

page 121

Publicly-traded corporations are a *separate social species.*
They make independent decisions, operate under a distinct
value system, and exhibit their own characteristic
behaviours.

page 131

The introduction of money in human interactions often
results in behaviours and outcomes which run contrary to our
established human values.

page 147

We've become *addicted* to a constantly growing economy,
and to get our short-term fix, we are willing to make some
very unhealthy choices.

page 150

Sustainability can only be achieved by recognizing and
adapting to *polarities* – cycles of conflicting forces that
create a dynamic equilibrium.

page 157

There are three objectives for an optimal group decision-
making system: *manageability, fairness,* and *effectiveness.*

page 165

Majority rule results in the best decisions only when the
population is sufficiently informed, interested, engaged, and
consulted – typically a rare combination.

page 170

Representative democracies favour decisions that produce
short-term benefits. Most long-term objectives are either
ignored, or leaders cannot stay in power long enough to
achieve them.

page 171

Representative democracies favour decisions that are
defensible, which introduces another social bias towards
number-based value systems.

page 172

Modern networking technology opens up a huge potential for
improved large group decision-making using participatory
democracy – a *wikiocracy*.

page 177

As *citizens*, we value social responsibility and a healthy
environment; as *consumers*, we want lower prices and more
selection; as *investors*, we want to profit from a continuously
growing economy.

page 184

Our internal *consumer* addresses immediate needs; our
investor plans for future needs; our *citizen* provides the
impulse for collaboration, empathy, moderation, and justice.

page 186

Free markets look after *consumers* and *investors*, but their
number-based value system renders them incapable of caring
for the values of *citizens*.

page 188

> The single most important role of governments is to represent *citizen* values, not the monetary-based *consumer* and *investor* values.
>
> *page 188*

> It is *our actions* as consumers and investors that sustain the cut-throat level of competition between corporations. The relentless drive for lower costs and higher profits comes from us, not from them.
>
> *page 190*

> Corporations are *not* citizens and should have no partici-pative role in government. The power of industry lobbies should never exceed the power of our regulatory government agencies.
>
> *page 191*

> Actions taken to improve humanity's prospects for survival will have negative *economic* consequences. The value of such actions will need to be measured on *other* scales.
>
> *page 197*

Index *(and Quotes)*

About the Author

Andrew Welch is a speaker, facilitator, disaster management leader, theatre director, designer, actor, handyman, experiential educator, town crier, and SAR instructor, to name a few of his (mostly volunteer) pursuits. He formed his first company (Caduceus Medical Software) in 1984, and now operates Intellact (www.intellact.ca), an entity whose projects are as diverse as Andrew's interests. He was most widely known for WattPlot, a software suite sold around the world for monitoring renewable energy systems (now free).

Andrew 'retired' just before reaching 40, when he learned from his father and others that retirement does not mean you have to stop working. Instead, it can mean that you stop doing what you don't want to do, you no longer take on long-term work commitments, and you are free to do your own thing for extended periods. Like writing a book. Or two.

www.TheValueCrisis.com

Also by Andrew Welch:

OUR

SECOND CHANCE

CHANGING COURSE AND
SOLVING THE VALUE CRISIS

ANDREW WELCH

The solution-packed sequel to The Value Crisis

Published by Captus Press
available from https://TheValueCrisis.com

Made in the USA
Middletown, DE
23 December 2022

18483556R00126